the Lazy Gourmet

the Lazy Gourmet

Susan Mendelson & Joey Cruz

Whitecap Books

Vancouver/Toronto

Edited by Elaine Jones
Proofread by Elizabeth McLean
Cover design by Peter Cocking
Interior design by Lisa Eng-Lodge
Cover photograph by Patrick Koslo
Inset photograph on cover by Derik Murray
Interior photographs by Greg Athans
Food styling by Joey Cruz
Food styling assisting by John Paskale

Printed and bound in Canada

Canadian Cataloguing in Publication Data

Mendelson, Susan, 1952-
  The Lazy Gourmet

  Includes index.
  ISBN 1-55110-966-2

  1. Cookery—British Columbia—Vancouver. 2. Lazy Gourmet Inc.
  (Restaurant) I. Title.
  TX945.5.L49M46 2000   641.5'09711'33   C99-910837-9

The publisher acknowledges the support of the Canada Council for the Arts
and the Cultural Services Branch of the Government of British Columbia for
our publishing program. We acknowledge the financial support of the
Government of Canada through the Book Industry Development Program
for our publishing activities.

Contents

Acknowledgments

It would not be possible to list all those who contributed ideas for this cookbook or made my life easier while I was engrossed in this process but heartfelt thanks go to my kitchen, bakery and operations staff. Your dedication and work ethic are both an inspiration and source of pride to me.

Special thanks go to Jenny Hui, my Kitchen Manager, for enduring my countless adjustments and revisions.

My gratitude also goes to my family: Dad—Reynaldo, Mom—Maria Natividad, brothers—Gabby and Alex, sister—Angela; whose love and support are always there for me.

— Joey Cruz

Many thank yous are in order for this cookbook. Joey Cruz has worked tirelessly for over a year preparing and testing these recipes for home use. Jenny Hui has worked with both Joey and me to type the original manuscript. Of course, this goes well beyond typing as Jenny had to decipher all of our notes and scribbles as well as to mathematically scale many of the recipes. Our pastry department, headed by Dana Blundell with Karen Bloodsworth, has made major contributions to the book. Magdi El-Gazar, our chief steward, has held it all together in the kitchen during the final stages of cookbook production. The rest of the team at The Lazy Gourmet have all contributed in some way to help create this book and I thank you all.

Most of my other cookbooks were written when I was single and had the time and energy to work 18-hour days. My family has been very supportive. I have to thank my husband, Jack Lutsky, who took over most weekends when I would steal time away from Mira and him to work on the book. Soleil, who is grown up, helped so much by also caring for Mira when I needed to work. Mira hardly knows that she's been neglected! She has also been wonderfully supportive, especially while helping me with the cookie section of the book! She is affectionately referred to by my staff as Madame Vice-President and she secretly enjoys it, although I'm not sure that she wants to work so hard when she grows up.

My twin sister, Lynn, who has been simultaneously working on a cookbook—*Chicken! Chicken! Chicken!*—has been a tremendous source of inspiration. We have shared anxieties and recipes and pushed each other along, much as we did when we worked on projects at school too many years ago. Rena and Freddie, as always, have been there as supports and friends. My mother-in-law and father-in-law, Joe and Miriam Lutsky, phone me regularly to tell me to make an appointment with myself for myself. My mother, Roz, who is a mother like no other, is my ultimate inspiration and I thank you for being there for me all the time.

— Susan Mendelson

Introduction

Perspective is an interesting thing. I started to write a cookbook almost 25 years ago and I was going to title it *The Lazy Gourmet Cookbook*. The original concept was to simplify classical recipes for people who wanted gourmet food but who were too "lazy" to follow all of the complicated steps in those early classical cookbooks.

I got slightly distracted. I started sharing recipes on CBC Radio and that turned into my first cookbook, *Mama Never Cooked Like This,* which was released 20 years ago. A friend and I started a small take-out gourmet food shop in Vancouver and we decided to use the name The Lazy Gourmet, because we would create gourmet food for people who were too lazy to make it themselves. The concept caught on and now 20 years later I find myself married with two children, a catering and restaurant business with over a hundred employees, and seven cookbooks under my belt. Now, I am finally writing *The Lazy Gourmet Cookbook*.

The cookbook is filled with recipes from the bistro and the catering company. Many of the recipes have been requested for years and we are finally parting with them. Many have been created by our chef, Joey Cruz, and contain his own special touches. Joey is not only a fabulous chef but also an inspiration to all those who work with him. He is an extraordinary team builder and everyone who knows him adores him. Joey has translated complicated procedures into simpler formats so that you can make all of these recipes in your homes.

We hope that you feel proud and excited to serve these recipes and that you'll make them part of your personal repertoire and traditions in your own families.

Enjoy!

—Susan Mendelson

hors d'oeuvres

Crêpe Fans
with Assorted Fillings

Makes 2 dozen

2	eggs	2
2	egg yolks	2
1½–1¾ cups	milk	360–420 mL
1 tsp.	salt	5 mL
1 tsp.	sugar	5 mL
⅞ cup	all-purpose flour, sifted	210 mL
⅔ cup	unsalted butter, melted	160 mL
1 recipe	your choice of fillings (facing page)	1 recipe

Have fun playing with any variation of this crêpe. You can vary the shape of the crêpes, as well as the fillings.

Beat the eggs and egg yolks, 1½ cups (360 mL) milk, salt and sugar in a mixing bowl.

Place the flour in a large mixing bowl and add the milk mixture. Whisk until a smooth batter is formed, adding more milk if the mixture is too thick. It should coat the back of a spoon.

Whisk in the melted butter.

To cook the crêpe, spray a 6-inch (15-cm) non-stick skillet with oil. Heat the skillet over medium to high heat. Pour approximately ¼ cup (60 mL) of batter into the pan and quickly swirl the pan to spread the batter evenly. Cook until the center is set and the bottom is light brown. Flip the crêpe over and lightly brown the other side. Transfer the cooked crêpe to a baking sheet to cool. Cook the remaining batter in the same way, to produce 12 crêpes about 5½ inches (14 cm) across.

Stack the crêpes, placing a sheet of parchment paper between each one. They can be wrapped and frozen until needed.

To assemble, cut the crêpes in half to create 24 semi-circle "fans." Lay a crêpe fan out on a clean surface with the flat side toward you.

Place a small amount of your choice of filling at the left edge of the fan.

Begin rolling the fan, starting on the left side. Fold the crêpe over the filling and continue rolling until a cone is formed. Prepare the rest of the crêpe fans in the same way.

Lox, Dill and Cream Cheese

½ cup	whipped cream cheese	120 mL
2¼ oz.	lox, cut into 24 ½-inch (1.2-cm) strips	65 g
24	sprigs dill	24

Spoon 1 tsp. (5 mL) of cream cheese onto each crêpe. Place a strip of lox and a sprig of dill on top.

Roasted Red Pepper and Chèvre

2 Tbsp.	chèvre	30 mL
6 Tbsp.	cream cheese	90 mL
1	large roasted red bell pepper, cut into 24 ½-inch (1.2-cm) strips (see Roasting Peppers, page 173)	1

Combine the chèvre and cream cheese, mixing well. Spoon 1 tsp. (5 mL) of the mixture onto each crêpe. Place a strip of red pepper on top.

Peking Duck and Hoisin

3 oz.	duck breast	85 g
	salt and black pepper to taste	
2 Tbsp.	hoisin sauce	30 mL
¾ cup	shredded green leaf lettuce	180 mL

Preheat the oven to 375°F (190°C).

Remove the skin from the duck breast. Place the skin on a baking sheet and bake until the skin is crispy, about 10–12 minutes. Remove from the oven and let cool.

Salt and pepper the duck breast. Using a hot sauté pan, sear the duck on both sides, about 3 minutes per side. Place in an oven-proof pan and bake for 12–15 minutes. Remove from the oven and let cool.

Slice the duck breast and skin into ½-inch (1.2-cm) slices. Toss with hoisin sauce. Place the duck strips and some lettuce onto the crêpe fans.

Steamed Mussels with Garlic, Roasted Fennel, Bell Peppers and Herbs

Serves 8

½ bulb	fennel, cut into thin strips	½ bulb
½	red bell pepper, cut into thin strips	½
½	green bell pepper, cut into thin strips	½
2½ Tbsp.	olive oil	37.5 mL
2 tsp.	garlic, minced	10 mL
1 cup	white wine	240 mL
1 cup	Tomato Sauce (page 107)	240 mL
2½ lbs.	mussels, bearded and washed	1.1 kg
2 tsp.	chopped mixed herbs (thyme, parsley, chives)	10 mL

The roasted vegetables in this recipe bring out the rich sweetness of the mussels. Use P.E.I. mussels if you can – they are particularly sweet and plump. Try this dish with your favorite Chardonnay.

Toss the fennel and pepper strips with 2 Tbsp. (30 mL) of the olive oil and place under the broiler, stirring occasionally, for about 5–7 minutes, until soft and lightly browned.

Sauté the garlic in the remaining olive oil for about a minute over low heat. Do not brown the garlic, as it will impart a bitter taste to the sauce. Add the wine and tomato sauce, then the mussels. Top with the roasted vegetables and cover the pan with a lid. Cook over medium heat until the mussels open, about 7–8 minutes. Sprinkle the herbs over top and cook for about a minute longer.

Serve immediately in a large bowl with plenty of crusty bread on the side.

Note: When cleaning the mussels, discard any that are open.

Thai Shrimp Salad on Jasmine Rice Cakes

Makes 2 dozen

1 cup	jasmine rice	240 mL
1¼ cups	water	300 mL
¼ cup	coconut milk	60 mL
½ lb.	fresh, cooked baby shrimp	225 g
½ cup	Thai Green Curry Sauce (page 83)	120 mL
½	medium red bell pepper, finely diced ½	
2 Tbsp.	chopped chives	30 mL

Wash and drain the rice. Cook the rice in a rice cooker with the water. To cook rice in a saucepan, place the rice and water in the pot, and bring to a boil. When "steam holes" appear, turn the heat to very low. Cover and finish cooking for about 15 minutes.

Scoop the cooked rice into a bowl. Quickly add the coconut milk and mix well. Place the rice on a baking sheet and flatten to ½ inch (1.2 cm). Wrap with clear plastic and store in the fridge for a minimum of 4 hours or overnight to set.

Using a ½-inch (1.2-cm) circular cutter, cut out 24 rounds. (You can also cut the rice cakes into small squares or triangles.)

Toss the baby shrimp and Thai curry sauce together.

Place about ½ Tbsp. (7.5 mL) of shrimp on top of each rice cake. Garnish with red peppers and chives.

A very elegant and flavorful hors d'oeuvre. The coconut milk binds the rice and gives it a gorgeous aroma. Leftover Thai Green Curry Sauce can be stored in the fridge for up to 10 days.

Ahi Tuna Crostinis with Wasabi Cream and Sun-dried Cherry Chutney

Makes 2 dozen

½ lb.	ahi tuna (call your local Japanese store), cut with the grain into strips, 1 x 1½ x 6 inch (2.5 x 3.8 x 15 cm)	225 g
	rock salt	
1 cup	buttermilk	240 mL
1 Tbsp.	wasabi powder	15 mL
½ cup	sour cream	120 mL
1	baguette	1

Simple and elegant, these can be put together at the last moment!

Cover the tuna completely with rock salt. Let sit in the fridge for one day. Remove the salt and discard.

Soak the tuna in buttermilk for about 1 hour. Slice it very thinly across the grain into pieces that will fit onto a crostini round. Set aside.

Mix the wasabi powder and sour cream until well blended. Set aside.

Preheat the oven to 275°F (135°C). Cut the baguette diagonally into 24 ½-inch (1.2-cm) slices. Place on a baking sheet and toast lightly in the oven. Generously spread the wasabi cream on each slice. Place the tuna on top. Garnish with the cherry chutney.

Sun-dried Cherry Chutney

1 cup	sun-dried cherries	240 mL
½ cup	sugar	120 mL
1 tsp.	ginger, minced	5 mL
1 cup	water	240 mL

Combine the sun-dried cherries, sugar, ginger and water in a saucepan. Bring to a boil. Simmer until thick, approximately 15 minutes.

Torta Basilica

Serves 8

¾ cup	sun-dried tomatoes	180 mL
½ cup	pine nuts, toasted (see Toasting Nuts, page 173)	120 mL
3 cups	whipped cream cheese	720 mL
½ cup	pesto	125 mL

The type of bowl chosen will form the shape of the basilica. We recommend a deep bowl, approximately 6-cup (1.5-L) size. Line the bowl with plastic wrap.

Place 3 whole sun-dried tomatoes in a star-burst pattern in the bottom of the bowl. Sprinkle 1 Tbsp. (15 mL) of the pine nuts around the tomatoes.

Julienne ½ cup (120 mL) of the sun-dried tomatoes and set aside. Purée the remaining sun-dried tomatoes. Blend thoroughly with about 1½ cups (360 mL) of cream cheese and set aside.

With a pastry bag, pipe half of the sun-dried tomato–cream cheese mixture around the bottom of the bowl to create the first layer. Spread half the pesto over top. Pipe about ¾ cup (180 mL) of the cream cheese on top of the pesto. Distribute the julienned tomatoes and the remaining pine nuts around the edges and over the cream cheese. Pipe on the remainder of the sun-dried tomato–cream cheese mixture. Spread the remainder of the pesto over top, and pipe on the remaining cream cheese. Cover with plastic wrap and place in the refrigerator for at least 2 hours, preferably overnight.

To server, invert the bowl onto a serving platter. Lightly tap the sides so the basilica slides out of the bowl. Remove the plastic wrap. Serve with crackers or baguettes.

This is a year-round favorite – refreshing in the summer and a comfort food in the cold winter. Experiment with your own decorative ideas for the top. It will definitely wow your guests. The recipe can be easily doubled. We use dried tomatoes for this; you can use oil-packed tomatoes, as long as you drain them well.

Almond Pine Cone Spread

Serves 8

1 lb.	cream cheese	455 g
1¾ oz.	blue cheese	50 g
1¾ oz.	chèvre	50 g
½ cup	capers, chopped	120 mL
½ cup	finely diced red onion	120 mL
1 Tbsp.	brandy	15 mL
4 cups	whole blanched almonds, toasted (see Toasting Nuts, page 173)	950 mL

This has always been a holiday special, but we've started to sell it year round due to its popularity. It has been called everything from a hedgehog to an armadillo to a porcupine by our customers — but we know what they mean when they order it!

Combine all the ingredients, except for the almonds. Mix until all the ingredients are well blended.

Shape into a pine cone.

Starting from the bottom, insert the almonds at a slight angle, forming neat rows so that it looks like one large pine cone. Serve with crackers or sliced baguettes.

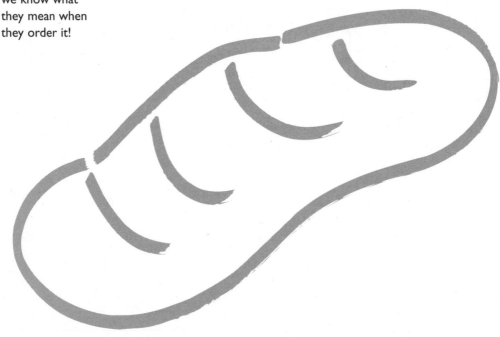

Brie-en-Croute with Reduced Maple Syrup and Toasted Walnuts

Serves 15 to 20

1 lb.	puff pastry	455 g
1	egg	1
2 Tbsp.	water	30 mL
2 lbs.	Brie cheese	900 g
1 cup	maple syrup	240 mL
½ cup	walnuts, coarsely chopped	120 mL

Divide the puff pastry into 2 balls. Roll each ball out to ¼-inch (.6-cm) thickness by 15 inches (38 cm) in diameter.

Whisk the egg and water together to make an egg wash. Brush one sheet of pastry with the egg wash. Place the Brie on top and brush with the egg wash. Place a second sheet of puff pastry on top of the Brie. Wrap the sides up and over the cheese. Decorate with extra puff pastry by shaping or cutting out designs. Brush the top and sides of the pastry with the egg wash. Place in the freezer for 1 hour.

Preheat the oven to 400°F (200°C). Bake the Brie for 30–45 minutes, or until the pastry is golden brown.

In a small pot, combine the maple syrup and walnuts. Bring to a boil, then turn down to a low simmer. Reduce to obtain a consistency similar to that of honey.

Place the baked Bried on a serving platter. Pour the maple syrup and walnuts over and around the Brie.

We started making the Brie-en-Croute almost 20 years ago, and often vary the recipe topping with fruits, nuts, pesto, etc. Have fun with the concept and make it your own!

Chèvre and Sun-dried Tomato Phyllo Purses

Makes 5 to 6 dozen

1 cup	sun-dried tomatoes, roughly chopped	240 mL
1 cup	whipped cream cheese	240 mL
1	egg, lightly whisked	1
¼ cup	chèvre	60 mL
1	1-lb. (454-g) package phyllo pastry, thawed	1
	olive oil	

Once you get the hang of phyllo, it is very easy to work with. Just remember to keep it covered with a damp tea towel when you're not working with it, as it tends to dry out very quickly. Cook only as many of these hors d'oeuvres as you can use. Freeze leftover unbaked phyllo purses and pull them out to bake when company arrives unexpectedly. Just place the frozen phyllo purses into a preheated oven.

In a bowl, mix together the sun-dried tomatoes, cream cheese, half the whisked egg and chèvre.

Lay one sheet of phyllo lengthwise on a clean surface. Brush with olive oil. Lay a second sheet on top and brush with olive oil, then a third sheet and brush with olive oil.

Cut the sheets in half horizontally and vertically to create 4 rectangular sheets. Then cut each sheet into 3 even columns, for a total of 12 columns.

Place ½–1 tsp. (2.5–5 mL) of the chèvre mixture at the bottom of each phyllo column. Fold the right corner to the left side of the phyllo column to form a triangle. Fold the triangle upwards. Then fold the left corner to the right side of the sheet again, forming a triangle. Fold the triangle upwards, and continue repeating the process until you reach the top of the phyllo column and a triangular purse is formed. Repeat with the remaining phyllo and filling.

Preheat the oven to 400°F (200°C). Brush the top of each purse with olive oil and place on baking sheets for 10–12 minutes, until golden brown.

Peking Duck on Polenta with Cranberry Chutney

Serves 8

4 oz.	duck breast, skin attached	113 g
1⅝ cups	milk	390 mL
1⅝ cups	water	390 mL
	pinch salt	
1 cup	cornmeal	240 mL
1 cup	cranberries	240 mL
½ cup	brown sugar	120 mL
½ cup	orange juice	120 mL

Preheat the oven to 375°F (190°C). Sear the duck in a sauté pan for about 3 minutes on each side. Place on a baking sheet and bake for 20 minutes. Remove and let cool. Cut into 24 ¼-inch (.6-cm) slices and set aside in the fridge.

In a small pot, bring the milk and water to a boil. Season with salt. Add the cornmeal and cook, stirring occasionally, for about 15 minutes. (Turn the heat down after about 5 minutes.) The cornmeal should be very thick, thicker than porridge. Pour onto a baking sheet and spread it out to form a ½-inch (1.2-cm) layer. Allow to set for 2 hours at room temperature. Using a 1-inch (2.5-cm) circular cutter, cut 24 rounds. Set aside.

To make the chutney, combine the cranberries, brown sugar and orange juice in a small pot. Bring to a boil. Cook until the liquid is reduced and the chutney has a thick, jam-like consistency. Set aside to cool.

Place a slice of duck breast on top of each polenta round and top with 1 tsp. (5 mL) chutney. Serve at room temperature.

Prepare this appetizer ahead of time and enjoy the party with your guests!

Quesadillas
with Three Fillings

Makes 4 dozen

24	6-inch (15-cm) soft tortillas	24
1	egg	1
2 Tbsp.	water	30 mL
1 recipe	your choice of fillings (below)	1 recipe
1 recipe	Salsa (page 171)	1 recipe

Preheat the oven to 375°F (190°C).

Lay 12 tortillas out on a clean surface. Combine egg and water and brush the egg wash on the tortillas with a pastry brush.

Evenly distribute your choice of filling, up to 5–6 Tbsp. (75–90 mL), on each tortilla.

Brush the other 12 tortillas with egg wash and place on top of the filled tortillas. Press down to flatten the filling.

Spray a baking sheet with vegetable spray, or oil lightly. Place quesadillas on the sheet and bake for 10–15 minutes, until the edges are slightly browned.

Cut each tortilla into 4 wedges. Serve with salsa, sour cream and guacamole.

Quesadillas are so versatile, lending themselves to almost any filling combination. We've found that these are the most popular. Our simple salsa recipe has endured for many years.

Triple Cheese Filling

1½ lbs.	whipped cream cheese	680 g
½ cup	red onion, finely diced	120 mL
1 cup	cilantro, roughly chopped	240 mL
¼ cup	jalapeño, roughly chopped	60 mL
½ cup	grated Cheddar cheese	120 mL
½ cup	grated Edam cheese	120 mL

In a food processor, blend all the ingredients until well combined. At this point, the filling may be stored in an airtight container in the fridge for 1 week.

Caramelized Onions, Gorgonzola, Yellow Peppers and Fontina Filling

1 recipe	Triple Cheese Filling	1 recipe
1½ oz.	Gorgonzola or blue cheese	42 g
1½ oz.	fontina cheese, grated	42 g
1	medium yellow bell pepper, roasted and cut into strips (see Roasting Peppers, page 173)	1
1 recipe	Caramelized Onions (page 59)	1 recipe

Combine the Triple Cheese Filling with Gorgonzola or blue cheese and fontina. Mix until well blended. At this point, the filling may be stored in an airtight container in the fridge for 1 week.

Evenly distribute the cheese filling, yellow pepper and caramelized onion on the tortillas.

Grilled Chicken, Brie and Artichoke Hearts Filling

2 cups	artichoke hearts	475 mL
¼ cup	olive oil	60 mL
4–5 oz.	boneless skinless chicken breast	113–140 g
1 recipe	Triple Cheese Filling	1 recipe
3½ oz.	Brie, cut into chunks	100 g

Preheat the oven to 350°F (175°C). Drain the artichoke hearts and chop them roughly. Toss with the olive oil and place on a baking sheet. Bake for 10 minutes, or until lightly brown. Remove from the oven and allow to cool.

Grill the chicken breast for 6–8 minutes per side over medium heat. Cool and cut into thin strips.

Evenly distribute the cheese filling over the tortillas. Top each with strips of chicken, artichoke hearts and Brie.

Vietnamese Salad Rolls with Joey's Peanut Hoisin Sauce

Makes 2 dozen

8 cups	water	2 L
½ bag	thin dried rice vermicelli noodles	½ bag
24	rice papers, triangular shape	24
½ cup	grated carrot	120 mL
1 cup	shredded lettuce	240 mL
1	whole papaya or mango, cut into ½-inch (1.2-cm) strips	1
8	green onions, cut into 3-inch (7.5-cm) pieces	8
¼ cup	Peanut Sauce (page 172)	60 mL
¼ cup	hoisin sauce	60 mL
2 Tbsp.	lemon juice	30 mL
1 Tbsp.	water	15 mL

Feel free to experiment with the vegetables and proteins in your fridge to make interesting rolls and use up leftovers. The rice papers and hoisin sauce are available in the Asian section of most grocery stores.

Bring the 8 cups (2 L) of water to a boil in a large pot. Add the rice noodles. Stir and cook for 5–8 minutes. Drain and rinse with cold running water. Using a pair of scissors, roughly cut up the noodles. Set aside.

Completely soak 3–4 rice papers in warm water for 30 seconds. Remove and lay the rice papers on a clean surface, pointed side away from you.

Place a pinch of rice noodles, carrots, lettuce and papaya or mango on the wide end of the rice paper. Fold the sides over the filling. Fold the bottom of the rice paper over the filling. Insert a piece of green onion along the edge of the fold, allowing it to stick out of the roll. Continue folding over to seal. Place on a serving plate.

Repeat with the remaining rice papers and filling.

For the peanut hoisin sauce, thoroughly blend the peanut sauce, hoisin sauce, lemon juice and water. Serve in a dipping bowl.

Crab and Mango Rolls with Citrus Sauce

Makes 2 dozen

8 cups	water	2 L
½ bag	thin dried rice vermicelli noodles	½ bag
24	rice papers, triangular shape	24
½ cup	grated daikon	120 mL
1 cup	shredded lettuce	240 mL
1	whole mango or papaya, cut into ½-inch (1.2-cm) strips	1
½ cup	crabmeat	120 mL
1 recipe	Citrus Sauce	1 recipe

Bring the water to a boil in a large pot, and add the rice noodles. Stir and cook for 5–8 minutes. Drain the noodles and rinse them with cold running water. Drain again. Using a pair of scissors, roughly cut up the noodles. Set aside.

Completely soak 3–4 rice papers in warm water for 30 seconds. Remove and lay the rice papers on a clean surface, pointed side away from you.

Place a pinch of rice noodles, daikon, lettuce, mango or papaya and crabmeat on the wide end of the rice paper. Fold the sides over the filling. Fold the bottom end of the rice paper over the filling and fold over again to seal. Place on a serving plate.

Repeat with the remaining rice papers and filling. Serve with Citrus Sauce.

Crab and mango rolls are a year-round delight. Feel free to use the fake crab. It's delicious and less than a quarter of the cost of real crab. Rice papers are available in the Asian section of most super-markets.

Citrus Sauce

¼ cup	vegetable oil	60 mL
3 Tbsp.	soy sauce	45 mL
½ cup	orange juice	120 mL
1 tsp.	lemon juice	5 mL
1 tsp.	sesame oil	5 mL
1 Tbsp.	finely chopped green onion	15 mL

Stir all the ingredients together and serve in a dipping bowl.

Chicken Satays with Spicy Peanut Sauce

Makes 2 dozen

1½ lbs.	**boneless skinless chicken breast, cut into 24 2-inch (5-cm) strips vegetable oil**	680 g
½ cup	**Peanut Sauce (page 172)**	120 mL

Soak 24 bamboo skewers in hot water for 5 minutes. Thread the chicken strips onto the skewers.

Brush the chicken with oil. Grill over medium-high heat until cooked, or place the skewers on baking sheets and bake for 10–15 minutes at 375°F (190°C).

Place the peanut sauce in a dipping bowl. Serve the chicken hot.

We soak the skewers to prevent them from burning on the grill. Be sure to place the chicken at the top of the skewer to make it easy for your guests to eat.

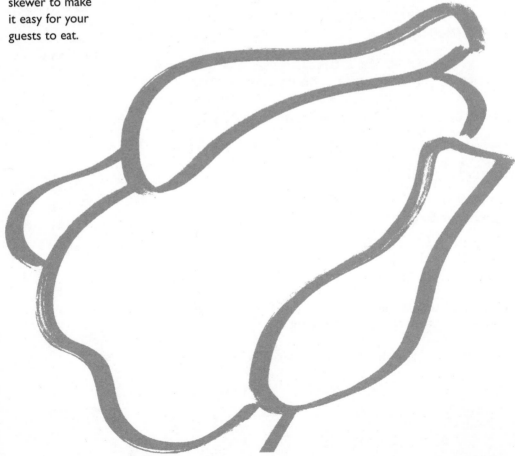

Prawn Satays Marinated with Cilantro Peanut Pesto

Makes 2 dozen

48	jumbo prawns, peeled and deveined	48
2	bunches cilantro	2
2 cups	basil	455 mL
1 cup	mint	240 mL
¼ cup	dry-roasted peanuts, ground	60 mL
3 Tbsp.	fish sauce	45 mL
2	cloves garlic	2
	vegetable oil (approximately ½ cup/120 mL)	

Soak 24 bamboo skewers in hot water for 5 minutes. Thread 2 prawns on each skewer. Place in a glass dish large enough to hold all the skewers.

In a food processor, purée the cilantro, basil, mint, ground peanuts, fish sauce and garlic. Add enough oil to form a thick paste. Coat the prawns with the cilantro peanut pesto until each prawn is well coated. Place in the fridge for 2 hours, turning once.

Preheat the oven to 375°F (190°C). Spray a baking sheet with vegetable oil, or lightly oil it. Place the skewers on the sheet and bake for 5–8 minutes.

These are so flavorful that you will not need a dipping sauce. Fish sauce is available in the Asian section of most grocery stores.

Blackened Beef Satays with Curry Mango Mayo

Makes 2 dozen

1½ lbs.	beef tenderloin, cut into 24 2- x ½-inch (5- x 1.2-cm) strips	680 g
1 recipe	Blackened Spice Mix (page 174)	1 recipe
½ cup	melted butter	120 mL

Soak 24 bamboo skewers in hot water for 5 minutes. Thread the tenderloin strips onto the skewers. Dredge in the spice mix.

The fruity mayonnaise in this unusual fusion of Cajun and Thai mellows the "heat" of the beef satays.

Place the skewers in a broiler pan and broil 4 inches (10 cm) from the element for about 3–4 minutes, turning once.

Brush the beef satays with butter to keep them from drying out.

Serve with the Curry Mango Mayo.

Curry Mango Mayo

1	ripe mango, peeled and pitted	1
2 Tbsp.	Thai red curry paste (found in most Asian supermarkets)	30 mL
½ cup	mayonnaise	120 mL

Purée the mango in a food processor or use a hand blender. Combine thoroughly with the curry paste and mayonnaise. Serve in a dipping bowl.

Toasted Coconut Prawns with Sun-dried Cherry Chutney

Makes 2 dozen

1½ cups	flour	360 mL
6	egg whites	6
1 tsp.	salt	5 mL
1 tsp.	pepper	5 mL
24	jumbo prawns, peeled and deveined	24
1½ cups	unsweetened coconut flakes	360 mL
2 cups	vegetable oil	475 mL

In a large mixing bowl, blend the flour, egg whites, salt and pepper to make a smooth batter.

Dip the prawns in the batter, then dredge them in coconut.

Heat the oil in a deep pot to 350°F (175°C). Deep-fry the prawns for 2 minutes. Remove with a slotted spoon and place on paper towel to drain.

Serve with Sun-dried Cherry Chutney (page 16).

Although we do not have a lot of fried items, these delicious prawns are the exception. Staff know that they have to hide them from me!

Crab Cakes with Fruit Salsa

Makes 3 dozen small cakes

⅓ cup	mayonnaise	75 mL
2	eggs	2
½ cup	chopped green onion	120 mL
¼ cup	finely diced red bell pepper	60 mL
¼ cup	finely diced celery	60 mL
2 Tbsp.	smooth Dijon mustard	30 mL
1	clove garlic	1
⅛ tsp.	cayenne	.5 mL
1 lb.	crabmeat, juice squeezed out	455 g
1 recipe	Fruit Salsa	1 recipe

Preheat the oven to 375° (190°C). Mix all the ingredients but the crabmeat and salsa until thoroughly combined. Fold the crabmeat into the vegetable-mayonnaise mixture.

With a 2-Tbsp. (30-mL) scoop, scoop the mixture onto well-greased baking pans. Flatten slightly. Bake for 5 minutes. Flip the cakes over and bake for 4 minutes longer, until lightly browned. Serve with Fruit Salsa.

Any crab will work with this recipe, so don't be turned off by the high price of Dungeness crab. The fruit salsa is very versatile and can be used as a sauce for any fish.

Fruit Salsa

¼	cantaloupe, cut into ¼-inch (.6-cm) dice	¼
¼	honeydew melon, cut into ¼-inch (.6-cm) dice	¼
2–3	slices pineapple, cut into ¼-inch (.6-cm) dice	2–3
½	small onion, cut into ¼-inch (.6-cm) dice	½
½	bunch cilantro, chopped	½
	juice of 1 lime	
2 Tbsp.	honey	30 mL
	salt and freshly ground black pepper to taste	
1 Tbsp.	red pepper flakes	15 mL

Mix all the ingredients together. Taste for seasoning and adjust if necessary. Chill until ready to serve.

Vegetarian Chopped Liver

Makes 2 cups (475 mL)

2 Tbsp.	vegetable oil	30 mL
1	12-oz. (340-mL) can green beans	1
1½	large onions, sliced or chopped	1½
3	hard-boiled eggs	3
½ cup	lightly toasted walnuts (See Toasting Nuts, page 173)	120 mL
1 Tbsp.	chopped fresh parsley	15 mL
1 tsp.	capers	5 mL
2 Tbsp.	mayonnaise	30 mL
	salt and black pepper to taste	

Drain the green beans and set aside. Heat the oil over medium heat and sauté the onions until they are caramelized lightly.

Put all the ingredients into a food processor and blend into a paste. Add a little more mayonnaise if needed to achieve the right consistency.

To serve, decorate with parsley and cherry tomatoes and provide a basket of crackers and sliced baguette.

We were once catering a kosher event in a synagogue. The client insisted on chopped liver but we couldn't get kosher liver. We made this recipe instead and the guests insisted that it was really chopped liver!

Roasted Garlic on Sicilian Flatbread

Serves 2

1	bulb garlic	1
1	pizza round (page 68)	1
2 Tbsp.	Basil Oil (page 176)	30 mL
2 Tbsp.	butter	30 mL
1 Tbsp.	brown sugar	15 mL
1	pear, halved	1
3 oz.	St. André or other triple-cream Brie	85 g

At the bistro, we serve this with a syrupy balsamic reduction drizzled over the top. But you can this "hot cheese course" in a lot less time by omitting that step.

Cut the top off the garlic bulb to expose the cloves. Rub the garlic with a bit of olive oil and roast in a preheated 375°F (190°C) oven for about 15 minutes. Set aside.

Heat the butter and brown sugar together in a saucepan to make a syrup. Cut the pear halves into slices without severing the top. Toss the pear in the syrup and place on a baking sheet. Roast in the oven for about 10–12 minutes. Keep warm.

Spread the basil oil over the pizza round and bake at 400°F (200°C) till crispy, about 10 minutes. Place the garlic on the flatbread and fan the pear beside it. Place the cheese on top of the pear. Return to the oven and heat through for another 4–5 minutes until the cheese starts to melt. Serve straight from the oven.

Back to front: Crêpe Fans (page 12), Ahi Tuna Crostinis with Wasabi Cream and Sun-dried Cherry Chutney (page 16) and Chicken Satays with Spicy Peanut Sauce (page 26).

soups

Wild Mushroom Soup

Serves 8

6 cups	mixed wild mushrooms (portobello, shiitake, oyster), sliced	1.5 L
3	shallots, finely chopped	3
2 Tbsp.	butter	30 mL
8 Tbsp.	flour	120 mL
6 cups	chicken or vegetable stock, heated	1.5 L
1 cup	whipping cream	240 mL
	salt and freshly ground white pepper to taste	
	cayenne to taste	
	chives, chopped	

The flavors of the mushrooms take over in this smooth and creamy soup.

Combine the sliced wild mushrooms and chopped shallots, and divide into 4 batches.

In a large pot with a wide bottom, sauté one batch of mushrooms and shallots in ½ Tbsp. (7.5 mL) of the butter over high heat. When the mushrooms start to color, add another ½ Tbsp. (7.5 mL) of butter and the second batch of mushrooms and shallots. When these are browned, continue with the remaining 2 batches, adding butter and browning the mushrooms lightly. This technique of cooking the mushrooms in batches is called "layering," as it creates different layers of flavor and texture in one ingredient.

Remove 1 cup (240 mL) of cooked mushrooms and shallots from the pan and set aside. Add the flour to the pan of remaining mushrooms and cook and stir over low heat until all the flour is absorbed.

Slowly whisk in the stock and bring to just a simmer. Add the whipping cream and return to a simmer. You may use half the whipping cream or substitute half and half if you want a soup that is lower in fat. Purée with a hand blender or food processor. Season to taste with salt, pepper and cayenne. Stir in the reserved mushrooms.

Ladle into 8 soup bowls and garnish with a generous sprinkling of chopped chives.

Roasted Red Pepper Soup

Serves 8

7	cloves garlic	7
6	roasted red peppers (see Roasting Peppers, page 173)	6
3	medium russet potatoes	3
8 cups	vegetable stock	2 L
	salt and freshly ground black pepper to taste	
2 Tbsp.	sherry vinegar	30 mL
½ cup	Crème Fraîche (page 177)	120 mL

Preheat the oven to 375°F (190°C).

Toss the garlic in a little olive oil. Place on a baking sheet and roast for about 10 minutes.

While the garlic is roasting, peel the potatoes and cut into slices about ¼ inch (.6 cm) thick. Place the peppers, potatoes, garlic and stock in a soup pot. Bring to a boil, then simmer about 20 minutes. Season with salt and pepper. Purée the soup in a food processor or with a hand blender. Stir in the sherry vinegar to finish.

Ladle into 8 soup bowls and garnish with a dollop of crème fraîche.

Garnished with a swirl of crème fraîche, this is a magnificent starter to a Spanish-theme dinner.

Chili-Corn Chowder Soup

Serves 8

1 cup	diced onion	240 mL
½ cup	diced celery	120 mL
2 Tbsp.	vegetable oil	30 mL
4 Tbsp.	flour	60 mL
2	red bell peppers, cored, seeded and diced	2
5 cups	corn kernels, fresh or frozen	1.25 L
2	russet potatoes, peeled and diced (cover with water until needed)	2
¼ tsp.	cayenne	1.2 mL
¼ tsp.	ground cumin	1.2 mL
¼ tsp.	chili powder	1.2 mL
6 cups	chicken or vegetable stock, heated	1.5 L
	salt and freshly ground white pepper to taste	
1 ½ cups	whipping cream	360 mL
	blue corn tortilla chips, for garnish	

Fresh corn is best, but frozen corn also works well to prepare a satisfying meal in a bowl any time of the year.

Sauté the onion and celery in the vegetable oil over medium heat until translucent, about 5 minutes. Add the flour and stir to form a light roux.

Combine the red peppers, corn and potatoes with the onion mixture. Add the cayenne, cumin and chili powder and stir until heated through.

Slowly whisk in the stock and bring to a simmer. Continue to simmer until the potatoes are cooked, about 15 minutes.

Season with salt and pepper. Stir in the whipping cream to finish.

Ladle into 8 soup bowls and top each bowl with a few blue corn tortilla chips.

Hot and Sour Soup

Serves 8

1 cup	julienned carrots	240 mL
1 cup	thinly sliced onions .	240 mL
1½ cups	shiitake mushrooms, thinly sliced	360 mL
1½ cups	oyster mushrooms, thinly sliced	360 mL
2 Tbsp.	vegetable oil	30 mL
	salt and freshly ground white pepper to taste	
2 Tbsp.	sambal oelek	30 mL
½ cup	rice wine vinegar	120 mL
8 cups	vegetable stock	2 L
1	8-oz. (225-g) package tofu, medium-firm, cut into ½-inch (1.2-cm) cubes	1
1 cup	chopped spinach	240 mL
3 Tbsp.	cornstarch	45 mL
3 Tbsp.	soy sauce	45 mL
2 Tbsp.	water	30 mL
½ cup	sliced green onions chili oil, for garnish	120 mL

In a soup pot, sauté the carrots, onions and both kinds of mush-rooms with the vegetable oil for about 5 minutes, until softened. Season lightly with salt and pepper.

Mix the sambal oelek with the rice vinegar and add it to the veg-etable mix. Pour in the stock and bring to a simmer. Add the tofu and spinach. Simmer gently for 15 minutes.

In a bowl, combine the cornstarch, soy sauce and water to make a slurry, or a paste. Blend the slurry into the soup, stirring constantly. Add the green onions and season with salt and pepper.

Ladle into 8 soup bowls and top each serving with a dash of chili oil.

A relatively new addition to our repertoire, this is already a big hit with our lun-cheon clients.

Vegetarian French Onion Soup

Serves 8

2 Tbsp.	butter	30 mL
2 Tbsp.	vegetable oil	30 mL
12	white onions, thinly sliced	12
3	cloves garlic, minced	3
3 Tbsp.	tomato paste	45 mL
10 cups	Vegetable Stock (page 168)	2.5 L
	salt and freshly ground white	
	pepper to taste	
½	loaf Italian or French bread	½
1 cup	grated Gruyère cheese	240 mL
½ cup	grated Parmesan cheese	120 mL

This is a wonderful comfort food. Although normally made with beef stock, this version is just as delicious and not as salty. Vegetarians are always grateful for this French classic turned veggie.

Heat the butter and oil in a heavy, wide-bottomed pot. Add the onions and cook over medium heat until they turn golden brown, about 12–15 minutes, stirring occasionally.

Stir in the garlic and tomato paste and cook another 7–10 minutes, stirring frequently. Add the vegetable stock and bring to a boil. Turn down to a simmer and cook for 20 minutes. Season to taste with salt and pepper.

While the soup is simmering, preheat the oven to 350°F (175°C). Cut the bread into 8 slices, about ¾ inch (2 cm) thick. Combine the two cheeses. Place the sliced bread on baking sheets and top with the cheese mixture. Toast the bread in the oven for about 5–7 minutes, until golden brown.

Ladle into 8 soup bowls and top each with a slice of toasted bread.

Watercress and Potato Soup

Serves 8

1½	white onions, coarsely chopped	1½
1	rib celery, coarsely chopped	1
1	carrot, coarsely chopped	1
2 Tbsp.	vegetable oil	30 mL
2 Tbsp.	butter	30 mL
7	yellow-fleshed potatoes, peeled and diced	7
8 cups	chicken or vegetable stock	2 L
2	bunches watercress, leaves and small stems only, coarsely chopped	2
1½ cups	whipping cream	360 mL
	salt and white pepper to taste	
	cayenne pepper	
½ cup	sour cream	120 mL
	watercress sprigs	

In a wide-bottomed pan over medium heat, sauté the onions, celery and carrot in the oil and butter until soft, about 5 minutes. Add the potatoes and pour in the stock. Bring to a boil, reduce to a simmer and cook for 10–15 minutes. Add the chopped watercress and whipping cream. Simmer slowly for 8–10 minutes.

Purée the soup with a hand blender or food processor. Pass through a strainer and season to taste with salt, white pepper and cayenne pepper.

Ladle into 8 soup bowls. Spoon a dollop of sour cream in the middle of each bowl and top with a sprig of watercress.

Here is a more assertive version of the classic leek and potato soup. Like leek and potato, it can also be served cold.

Roasted Tomato and Fennel Soup

Serves 8

15	Roma tomatoes, cut in half and seeded	15
1 cup	chopped fresh fennel	240 mL
3	cloves garlic, peeled	3
1	onion, peeled and chopped	1
4 Tbsp.	olive oil	60 mL
8 cups	Vegetable Stock (page 168)	2 L
1 Tbsp.	honey	15 mL
2 Tbsp.	balsamic vinegar	30 mL
	salt and freshly ground black pepper to taste	
4 Tbsp.	Parsley Oil (page 175)	60 mL
4 Tbsp.	extra virgin olive oil	60 mL

This intensely flavored soup is excellent as a light lunch or supper with our ciabatta bread, which is also available in Italian bakeries.

Preheat the oven to 400°F (200°C).

Combine the tomatoes, fennel, garlic cloves and onion in a mixing bowl. Add the olive oil and toss to coat.

Spread the vegetables onto 2 rimmed baking sheets and roast in the oven for 25–30 minutes, turning the vegetables at least once, until they are soft and browned.

Combine the vegetables and stock in a soup pot. Bring to a boil and simmer slowly for 10–15 minutes.

Blend the honey and balsamic vinegar together and stir into the soup.

Purée the soup with a hand blender or in a food processor. Season to taste with salt and pepper.

Ladle into 8 soup bowls and drizzle ½ Tbsp. (7.5 mL) each of parsley oil and extra virgin olive oil over the soup.

Chicken Lemon Soup with Orzo

Serves 8

This is a bit of a challenge to make, as you have to add the lemon-egg mixture, called a "liaison," to the base without turning it into egg-drop soup, with bits of cooked egg floating about. But the results are well worth the effort.

1½ lbs.	boneless chicken breast, diced	680 g
2	onions, diced	2
4 Tbsp.	vegetable oil	60 mL
8 cups	chicken stock	2 L
3 cups	cooked orzo	720 mL
1 tsp.	freshly chopped oregano	5 mL
	salt and freshly ground white pepper to taste	
3	eggs, separated	3
	juice of 2 lemons	
¼ cup	whipping cream	60 mL
	minced parsley, for garnish	

In a large pot over medium heat, sauté the diced chicken and onions in vegetable oil for 10 minutes.

Add the chicken stock and bring to a boil. Simmer slowly for about 15–20 minutes. Stir in the cooked orzo and fresh oregano. Season to taste with salt and white pepper.

In a large bowl, whip the egg whites to soft peaks. Fold in the egg yolks, lemon juice and whipping cream.

Add about ½ cup (120 mL) of the soup to the egg mixture and stir vigorously. Repeat 3–4 more times. This tempers the egg mixture, or liaison. Fold the liaison into the soup and stir.

Ladle into 8 soup bowls and sprinkle each serving with minced parsley.

To cook 3 cups (720 mL) of orzo, you will need at least 9 cups (2.25 L) of water. Add about 1½ Tbsp. (22 mL) of salt and 3 Tbsp. (45 mL) of vegetable oil. When the water is at a rolling boil, add 1½ cups (360 mL) orzo.

Stir occasionally with a wooden spoon and cook until it is *al dente*, or firm to the bite, about 8 minutes. Drain the orzo and it is ready to be used.

Green Vegetable Minestrone

Serves 8

4 Tbsp.	olive oil	60 mL
2	whole onions, coarsely diced	2
1	rib celery, coarsely diced	1
8 cups	vegetable stock	2 L
3	whole potatoes, peeled and coarsely diced	3
2 cups	sliced green beans	475 mL
1½ cups	chopped savoy cabbage	360 mL
2 cups	broccoli florets	475 mL
2 cups	diced zucchini	475 mL
2 cups	cooked white beans	475 mL
½ cup	Pesto (page 171)	120 mL
	salt and freshly ground white pepper to taste	

This is a terrific hearty soup. Served with a good bread, it's a meal in itself.

Heat the olive oil in a soup pot and sauté the onions and celery over medium heat.

Pour in the vegetable stock and add the potatoes. Bring to a boil and simmer for 12–15 minutes. Add the green beans and cabbage. Simmer slowly for 8–10 minutes, then add the broccoli, zucchini and white beans.

Stir in the pesto. Season to taste with salt and white pepper, and stir thoroughly to combine all ingredients. Bring to a boil for about 1 minute and remove from the heat.

Ladle into 8 soup bowls and serve with fresh bread.

salads

Oriental Scallop Salad with Citrus Dressing

Serves 8

2	carrots, julienned	2
1	daikon, julienned	1
½	head napa cabbage or sui choy, shredded	½
1 cup	rice wine vinegar	240 mL
4 Tbsp.	sugar	60 mL
1 Tbsp.	grated ginger	15 mL
	salt and freshly ground black pepper to taste	
24	large scallops	24
3 Tbsp.	white wine	45 mL
4 Tbsp.	olive oil	60 mL
1 tsp.	salt	5 mL
1 Tbsp.	coarse black pepper	15 mL
8 cups	mixed greens	2 L
5 cups	deep-fried rice vermicelli	1.25 L
	ketjap manis (sweet soy sauce)	
½ cup	Citrus Dressing	120 mL

The vermicelli noodles make a very dramatic presentation. I adore scallops but you can substitute large prawns. You will have leftover dressing but it will keep for 2–3 weeks in the fridge. Use it as a dressing with any salad you like.

In a glass dish, toss the carrots, daikon and cabbage or sui choy with the rice wine vinegar, sugar and ginger. Season with salt and pepper. Allow to sit in the refrigerator for approximately 1 hour. Drain off the marinade and return the vegetables to the fridge until needed.

In a bowl, toss the scallops with the wine, olive oil, salt and pepper. In a sauté pan over high heat, pan-fry the scallops until a crispy crust is formed, about 3 minutes on each side. Set aside.

Place the mixed greens in the center of a large platter and drizzle with Citrus Dressing. Drizzle the sweet soy sauce generously over the greens. Place the fried vermicelli on top. Evenly distribute the scallops and marinated vegetables around the plate and serve.

Citrus Dressing

3 Tbsp.	lemon zest	45 mL
1 cup	lemon juice	240 mL
1	clove garlic, sliced	1
3	1-inch (2.5-cm) pieces ginger, sliced	3
1 Tbsp.	brown sugar	15 mL
	honey to taste	
¾ cup	canola oil	180 mL
¾ cup	olive oil	180 mL

In a saucepan, combine the lemon zest, lemon juice, garlic, ginger and brown sugar. Bring to a boil, then simmer over medium heat until the mixture is reduced by half.

Remove from the heat and mix in honey to the desired sweetness. Allow to cool to room temperature.

Purée the lemon mixture in a blender. With the blender running, slowly add both oils until the dressing achieves a creamy texture.

Lazy Gourmet Niçoise Salad

Serves 8

2–3	heads romaine lettuce, torn into bite-size pieces	2–3
1 lb.	green beans, blanched	455 g
½ cup	sliced black olives	120 mL
1 recipe	Herb Vinaigrette	1 recipe
8	hard-boiled eggs	8
1	4–6 oz. (113–170 g) can flaked tuna, drained	1

In a large bowl, combine the romaine, green beans, olives and herb vinaigrette. Toss well. Cut the eggs in half lengthwise or dice, and arrange on top of the vegetables. Flake the tuna over the salad.

Herb Vinaigrette

¼ cup	white wine vinegar	60 mL
1 Tbsp.	chopped herbs (rosemary, chives, thyme or basil)	15 mL
1 Tbsp.	honey	15 mL
1 tsp.	Dijon mustard	5 mL
¾ cup	olive oil	180 mL
	salt and freshly ground black pepper to taste	

Blend the vinegar, herbs, honey and Dijon mustard. Slowly whisk in the olive oil until an emulsion has formed. Season with salt and pepper.

This is a very filling and well-balanced salad. If you're dieting, eat only the egg whites and reduce the quantity of the dressing.

Spinach, Portobello and Swiss Cheese Salad with Roasted Garlic Dressing

Serves 8

8	portobello mushrooms, stems and gills removed	8
½ cup	balsamic vinegar	120 mL
2 tsp.	salt	10 mL
1 Tbsp.	black pepper	15 mL
12 cups	baby spinach	3 L
1 recipe	Roasted Garlic Dressing	1 recipe
1 cup	grated Swiss cheese	240 mL

Preheat the oven to 350°F (175°C). In a shallow dish, marinate the mushrooms with the balsamic vinegar, salt and pepper for 10–15 minutes. Place the portobellos on a baking sheet and bake for 10 minutes, or until tender. Remove and let cool.

Arrange the spinach leaves on a platter and pour the garlic dressing over. Arrange the mushrooms (sliced or left whole) around the dish. Sprinkle the Swiss cheese over the spinach.

This is an end-of-the-century variation of the popular spinach salad from Mama Never Cooked Like This.

Roasted Garlic Dressing

10	cloves garlic	10
	canola oil	
¼ cup	balsamic vinegar	60 mL
1 Tbsp.	smooth Dijon mustard	15 mL
¾ cup	olive oil	180 mL

Preheat the oven to 350°F (175°C). Toss the garlic cloves in the canola oil. Place in a piece of foil and seal. Roast in the oven for 20–25 minutes, or until the garlic has softened. Allow to cool.

In a bowl, combine the roasted garlic, balsamic vinegar and Dijon mustard. Mash until the garlic is puréed. Slowly whisk in the olive oil, until dressing is well blended and smooth.

Hearts of Romaine Salad

Serves 8

1	egg	1
2 Tbsp.	capers	30 mL
4	cloves garlic	4
¼ cup	red wine vinegar	60 mL
1 Tbsp.	Dijon mustard	15 mL
¾ cup	olive oil	180 mL
	salt and freshly ground black pepper to taste	
8 cups	romaine hearts, torn into bite-size pieces	2 L
1 cup	Herbed Croutons	240 mL
½ cup	grated Parmesan cheese (Reggiano or Padano)	120 mL
½	medium red onion, sliced into ¼-inch (.6-cm) rings	½

Lots of flavor in this '90s version of the classic Caesar. You can substitute balsamic for red wine vinegar if you want even more taste.

To make the dressing, place the egg in boiling water for 90 seconds. Remove and set aside. In a food processor or blender, blend the capers, garlic, red wine vinegar, Dijon mustard and the coddled egg. With the machine running, slowly pour in the olive oil, until the mixture becomes thick and creamy. Season with salt and pepper.

To serve the salad, toss together the romaine, croutons, grated cheese and dressing. Pile high on a serving plate and arrange the onion rings around the salad. Sprinkle more Parmesan cheese on top, if desired.

Herbed Croutons

¼ cup	olive oil	60 mL
3 Tbsp.	chopped mixed fresh herbs (rosemary, basil, thyme, oregano)	45 mL
2 tsp.	salt	10 mL
1 tsp.	black pepper	5 mL
1 cup	day-old bread, cubed	240 mL

Preheat the oven to 350°F (175°C).

Mix the oil, herbs, salt and pepper together. Toss with the cubed bread in a bowl. Spread the croutons on a baking sheet and bake for 5–10 minutes, turning occasionally, until golden brown.

Shanghai Noodle Salad

Serves 8

6 oz.	cooked Shanghai noodles	170 g
5 Tbsp.	oil	75 mL
5 Tbsp.	honey	75 mL
2 Tbsp.	sesame oil	30 mL
3 Tbsp.	rice wine vinegar	45 mL
3 Tbsp.	soy sauce	45 mL
1½ tsp.	freshly grated ginger	7.5 mL
2 Tbsp.	peanut butter (unsweetened, smooth)	30 mL
1 tsp.	sambal oelek	5 mL
½	head napa cabbage or sui choy, shredded	½
4	bunches green onion, cut on the diagonal into ½-inch (1.2-cm) pieces	4
2	small carrots, julienned	2
1	medium red bell pepper, julienned	1
½ cup	dry-roasted peanuts, crushed	120 mL

Refresh the noodles by dropping them in boiling water for about 3 minutes. Drain the noodles and rinse under cold running water.

In a blender, thoroughly combine the oil, honey, sesame oil, vinegar, soy sauce, ginger, peanut butter and sambal oelek.

Place the noodles, cabbage, green onions, carrots, red pepper and peanuts into a bowl. Pour the dressing over and toss evenly.

This is a great salad to take to a summer picnic! Shanghai noodles are available in the refrigerated case at Asian grocery stores.

Southwest Corn, Barley, Red Pepper and Jicama Salad

Serves 8

½ cup	vegetable oil	125 mL
1 Tbsp.	minced garlic	15 mL
7 cups	corn	1.75 L
4 cups	raw pearl barley	1 L
6 cups	boiling water	1.5 L
2	medium jicama, cut into ¼-inch (.6-cm) dice	2
1	medium red bell pepper, cut into ¼-inch (.6-cm) dice	1
1 recipe	Spicy Orange Vinaigrette	1 recipe

This recipe is a wonderful combination of textures and flavors.

In a sauté pan, heat the oil and garlic over low to medium heat. Add the corn and sauté for about 2 minutes. Allow to cool.

Cook the barley in boiling water until soft, approximately 20–25 minutes, or until it reaches the desired consistency, adding more water if necessary. Drain and rinse under cold running water.

Combine the corn, barley, jicama and red pepper in a bowl. Toss with the dressing. Store in the refrigerator for at least an hour or overnight, to blend the flavors.

Spicy Orange Vinaigrette

½ cup	orange juice	120 mL
¼ cup	white wine vinegar	60 mL
	juice of 1 lime	
2 Tbsp.	chipotle chiles	30 mL
2 Tbsp.	chopped cilantro	30 mL
1 tsp.	ground cumin	5 mL
¾ cup	canola oil	180 mL
	salt and freshly ground black pepper to taste	

Using a blender or food processor, blend together the orange juice, white wine vinegar, lime juice, chipotles, cilantro and cumin. While still blending, slowly add in the oil until the dressing is creamy. Season with salt and pepper.

Strawberry Romaine Spinach Salad with Raspberry Poppyseed Dressing

Serves 8

6 cups	baby spinach	1.5 L
6 cups	romaine, cut into bite-size pieces	1.5 L
1 pint	strawberries, quartered	500 mL
½	small red onion, cut into ¼-inch (.6-cm) slices	½
1 recipe	Raspberry Poppyseed Dressing	1 recipe

Toss the spinach, romaine, strawberries and onion together in a large bowl. Drizzle with the dressing just before serving.

Raspberry Poppyseed Dressing

½ cup	mayonnaise	120 mL
4 Tbsp.	raspberry vinegar	60 mL
¼ cup	sugar	60 mL
¼ cup	milk	60 mL
2 Tbsp.	poppyseeds	30 mL

Thoroughly mix all ingredients together with a whisk.

The beauty of this salad is that both adults and kids adore it. It's probably our most popular catered salad!

Sweet Lettuce with Candied Pecans, Pears and Roquefort Dressing

Serves 8 to 10

1	head butter lettuce	1
1	small head red leaf lettuce	1
4 Tbsp.	Roquefort, Gorgonzola or blue cheese	60 mL
2	medium Bosc pears, peeled and sliced	2
½ cup	light oil	120 mL
3 Tbsp.	balsamic vinegar	45 mL
¼ tsp.	salt	1.2 mL
1	clove garlic, minced	1
1 recipe	Candied Pecans	1 recipe

Thanks to Paige Grunberg for sharing this recipe. This is a very festive salad, but be sure to cut the pears at the last minute. And don't leave the pecans on the counter for your guests to nibble at before dinner or you'll have none left for the salad!

Wash and dry the lettuce, and tear it into bite-size pieces. Place the lettuce in a bowl.

To make the dressing, combine the oil, vinegar, salt and garlic.

Crumble the cheese over the lettuce, add the pears and gently toss. Pour the dressing over the salad. Scatter the pecans over top.

Creamy Gorgonzola Variation

For an alternate taste, try this creamy gorgonzola dressing that we use in the bistro.

½ cup	mayonnaise	120 mL
½ cup	sour cream	120 mL
1 tsp.	Worcestershire sauce	5 mL
1 Tbsp.	sherry vinegar	15 mL
1 Tbsp.	sugar	15 mL
1	clove garlic, minced	1
	salt and cracked black pepper to taste	
3 oz.	Gorgonzola, Roquefort or blue cheese	85 g

Mix all the ingredients together, except for the cheese. Crumble the cheese into the dressing.

Candied Pecans

½ cup	pecans	120 mL
¼ cup	sugar	60 mL
½ tsp.	freshly ground black pepper	2.5 mL

Heat the pecans in a skillet over medium heat until they are hot, about 3 minutes. Toss to prevent burning.

Mix the sugar and pepper and toss half the mixture over the pecans. Reduce the heat slightly. Now watch the pan and don't do anything until the sugar begins to melt, then toss with a wooden spoon.

Add the rest of the sugar mixture and continue mixing until all the pecans are covered with caramelized sugar.

Pour the pecans onto a plate and let cool. Separate the nuts when cooled. (The candied nuts also freeze beautifully.)

Asian Slaw

Serves 8

½	head shredded white cabbage	½
½	head shredded red cabbage	½
4	medium carrots, julienned	4
1 recipe	Citrus Dressing	1 recipe
¼ cup	toasted sesame seeds	60 mL

In a mixing bowl, combine the cabbages and carrots.

Toss the vegetables with half the dressing. Taste and add more dressing if desired.

Just before serving, sprinkle sesame seeds over the salad.

A crunchy addition to any meal. It can be low-fat if you cut down on the dressing.

Citrus Dressing

6 Tbsp.	soy sauce	90 mL
2 Tbsp.	Worcestershire sauce	30 mL
1⅓ cups	orange juice	320 mL
2 Tbsp.	lemon juice	30 mL
¼ cup	chopped parsley	60 mL
⅔ cup	olive oil	160 mL

Mix the soy sauce, Worcestershire sauce, orange juice, lemon juice and parsley. Slowly whisk in the olive oil.

Mesclun Greens with Red Pepper, Chèvre and Macadamia Nuts

Serves 8

12 cups	mixed greens	3 L
1	red bell pepper, cut into	1
	¼-inch (.6-cm) slices	
4 oz.	macadamia nuts, toasted	113 g
	(see Toasting Nuts, page 173)	
6 oz.	chèvre	170 g
4 oz.	pickled ginger with juice	113 g
3	cloves garlic	3
1	whole jalapeño pepper, stemmed	1
1	½-inch (1.2-cm) piece baby	1
	ginger, peeled	
1 Tbsp.	sambal badjak	15 mL
½ cup	rice wine vinegar	120 mL
1 cup	light oil	240 mL
1	bunch cilantro	1

Wash the greens and put them into a bowl. Toss with the peppers.

Coarsely chop the macadamia nuts. Set aside.

Gently break the chèvre into chunks. Roll into 24 1-inch (2.5-cm) balls, then roll the balls in the macadamia nuts. Flatten into 1½-inch (3.8-cm) disks.

For the dressing, put all the remaining ingredients into a blender and process on high until everything is well puréed. Pour ¼ to ⅓ of the dressing over the salad. The rest will keep in the fridge for up to 2 weeks.

Arrange the salad on 8 serving plates and garnish each plate with 3 macadamia-chèvre disks. For a buffet, gently toss the salad with the chèvre disks. For a variation, warm the chèvre disks for 30 seconds in a 325°F (165°C) oven and gently spoon them onto the salad plates before just serving.

If this is not the best salad you've ever tasted, send me your recipe! The pickled ginger and sambal badjak can be found in most large supermarkets or the Asian section of your local store.

Thai Spinach Salad

Serves 6 to 8

1	3-oz. (85-mL) package enoki mushrooms	1
10 oz.	baby spinach	285 g
1 cup	very fresh bean sprouts	240 mL
1	medium yellow bell pepper, thinly sliced	1
½ cup	toasted slivered almonds	120 mL
3 Tbsp.	freshly squeezed lime juice	45 mL
2 Tbsp.	brown sugar	30 mL
1 Tbsp.	fish sauce	15 mL
½ tsp.	Chinese chili sauce	2.5 mL
2 tsp.	finely minced fresh ginger	10 mL
¼ cup	minced green onion	60 mL
¼ cup	minced fresh mint	60 mL
2 Tbsp.	minced basil	30 mL
½ tsp.	freshly grated nutmeg	2.5 mL
¼ cup	canola oil	60 mL

This is "fusion food" at its best — a combination of Asian herbs, spices and vegetables, mixed with local produce!

Cut off the dirty stem ends of the enoki mushrooms. Separate them into threads. Combine them with the spinach, bean sprouts, yellow peppers and almonds in a salad bowl.

Combine the remaining ingredients in a blender; process on medium speed for 15–20 seconds, until puréed. Pour the dressing over the salad and toss just before serving.

burgers, sandwiches & pizzas

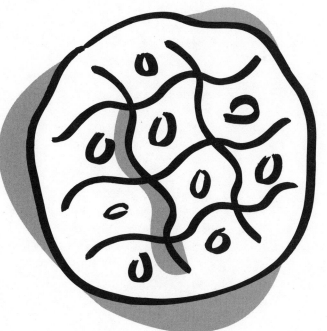

Lazy Gourmet Award-Winning Burgers with All the Trimmings

Makes 8 burgers

5 lbs.	ground beef	2.25 kg
½ cup	dry bread crumbs	120 mL
½	medium white onion, cut into ¼-inch (.6-cm) dice	½
1	egg	1
1½ Tbsp.	salt	22.5 mL
1 Tbsp.	freshly ground white pepper	15 mL
8	pieces white cheddar, each 1 inch (2.5 cm) square and ¼-inch (.6-cm) thick	8
8	kaiser buns	8
½ cup	Caramelized Onions	120 mL
½ cup	Barbecue Sauce (page 174)	120 mL
1 recipe	Chipotle Sauce	1 recipe
1 recipe	Spicy Spinach	1 recipe
16	slices tomatoes (optional)	16
8	slices pickle (optional)	8

People have been known to drive from far away for this tasty and unique burger.

In a bowl, combine the beef, bread crumbs, onion, egg, salt and pepper. Divide into 8 balls.

Divide each ball in half and shape into two patties. Place a piece of cheese in the center of one and top with the second patty. Form the two into one solid patty, ensuring that the cheese is not exposed. Repeat with the remaining 7 balls.

Pan-fry the burgers in a hot sauté pan. Cook each side for about 5 minutes, or until the burgers are no longer pink in the center.

Toast the buns lightly. On the bottom half of the bun, spread 1 Tbsp. (15 mL) caramelized onions. Place the patty on top and add 1 Tbsp. (15 mL) barbecue sauce and 1 Tbsp. (15 mL) chipotle sauce. Top with the spicy spinach, tomatoes and pickles if desired, and the top of the bun. Serve with chips or fries.

Caramelized Onions

Makes 1½ cups (360 mL)

2 Tbsp.	butter	30 mL
4	medium red onions, thinly sliced	4
1 Tbsp.	brown sugar	15 mL
½ Tbsp.	red wine vinegar	7.5 mL

In a sauté pan, melt the butter. Add the onions and brown sugar. Cook over low to medium heat, stirring occasionally, until very soft, about 10 minutes. Add the red wine vinegar. Continue cooking for 5 minutes.

Chipotle Sauce

1 Tbsp.	chipotle chiles, puréed	15 mL
½ cup	sour cream	120 mL
	juice of ¼ lemon	

Place the chipotles, sour cream and lemon juice in a food processor or blender and process until puréed.

Spicy Spinach

2 tsp.	chili oil	10 mL
2 cups	baby spinach	475 mL

In a sauté pan, heat the chili oil. Add the spinach and cook until wilted.

Lazy Gourmet's Award-Winning Veggie Burgers

Makes 8 burgers

1 lb.	carrots, grated	455 g
¾ lb.	orange Cheddar cheese, grated	340 g
¼ cup	dried parsley	60 mL
½ cup	soy sauce	120 mL
2 cups	fresh bread crumbs	475 mL
5	eggs	5
1 cup	sunflower seeds	240 mL
1 cup	chopped walnuts	240 mL
2–3 Tbsp.	vegetable oil	30–45 mL
8	kaiser buns	8
1 recipe	Spicy Spinach (page 59)	1 recipe
16	slices tomato (optional)	16
8	slices pickle (optional)	8
1 recipe	Caramelized Onions (page 59)	1 recipe
1 recipe	Chipotle Sauce (page 59)	1 recipe
1 recipe	Barbecue Sauce (page 174)	1 recipe

The recipe has been a huge favorite for many years. Lots of texture combined with a rich flavor makes it a satisfying alternative to the beef burger.

Mix the carrots, cheese, parsley, soy sauce, bread crumbs, eggs, sunflower seeds and walnuts together. If the mixture is too wet, add more bread crumbs. If the mixture is too dry, add an egg.

Divide into 8 balls and shape into patties.

In a hot sauté pan, fry the patties in vegetable oil until crispy all around, about 4 minutes on each side.

Toast the buns. Arrange some spicy spinach and tomatoes and pickles, if desired, on the top half of the buns. Spread caramelized onions on the bottom half of the buns. Place the burgers on the onions and spread with chipotle sauce and barbecue sauce. Enjoy!

Basil-Marinated Grilled Chicken Sandwiches with Bocconcini and Pesto Mayonnaise

Makes 8 sandwiches

8	4-oz. (113-g) boneless skinless chicken breasts	8
1 cup	Basil Oil (page 176)	240 mL
1 Tbsp.	Pesto (page 171)	15 mL
⅓ cup	mayonnaise	80 mL
16	slices your favorite bread (sourdough is excellent)	16
16	tomato slices, ¼ inch (.6 cm) thick	16
16	whole basil leaves	16
8	pieces bocconcini, each cut into 3 slices softened butter	8

Preheat the oven to 350°F (175°C). In a shallow pan, marinate the chicken pieces in the basil oil for 30 minutes.

Brown both sides of each chicken piece in a hot pan, about 2 minutes per side. Place in an ovenproof pan and bake for 10 minutes. Cut into thin slices.

Mix the pesto and mayonnaise together. Spread about 1 tsp. (5 mL) on each slice of bread.

To assemble the sandwiches, lay out 8 slices of bread and several slices of chicken, 2 tomato slices, and 3 pieces of bocconcini on each. Top with 2 basil leaves and another bread slice.

Butter the outsides of the sandwiches.

Place the sandwiches in a sauté pan over medium heat. Cook until both sides are golden brown and the cheese has melted, turning once (lower the heat if necessary to prevent burning).

A great combination of flavors. A panini machine makes this easier, but any sandwich press—even a sauté pan—will also do. If you can, place something flat on top of the sandwich and weigh it down for an effect similar to the press.

Grilled Portobello Mushroom and Goat Cheese Sandwiches

Makes 8 sandwiches

8	portobello mushrooms	8
½ cup	balsamic vinegar	120 mL
	salt and freshly ground black pepper to taste	
4	red bell peppers, halved lengthwise and core and seeds removed	4
½ cup	goat cheese	120 mL
2 Tbsp.	chopped fresh herbs (thyme, basil, rosemary)	30 mL
8	squares focaccia bread, sliced in half	8

Marinate the mushrooms with the balsamic vinegar, salt and pepper for 20 minutes. Grill the mushrooms and peppers until tender, about 4 minutes per side, over medium heat. Allow to cool.

Mix the goat cheese and herbs. Spread a generous amount of the mixture on the bottom half of each focaccia square. Place a portobello mushroom and a pepper half on the goat cheese, and top with the remaining focaccia.

Butter the outsides of the sandwiches.

In a sauté pan, cook the sandwiches over medium heat, turning once, until both sides of each sandwich are golden brown and the cheese has melted. (Lower the heat, if necessary, to prevent burning.)

The combination of rich goat cheese, meaty portobellos and sweet roasted peppers make this hearty sandwich an ideal meal before a sporting activity—not too heavy but hits the spot.

Roast Vegetables Sandwich

Makes 8 sandwiches

	vegetable oil	
2	**Japanese eggplant, cut diagonally into ¼-inch (.6-cm) slices**	2
2	**zucchini, cut diagonally into ¼-inch (.6-cm) slices**	2
5	**red bell peppers, halved lengthwise and core and seeds removed**	5
½ cup	**mayonnaise**	120 mL
16	**slices your favorite bread**	16
3	**fresh tomatoes, sliced**	3
1 cup	**arugula**	240 mL
8	**slices fontina cheese**	8

Brush lightly with oil and grill the eggplant for 4 minutes, zucchini for 3 minutes, and peppers for 4 minutes over low to medium heat. Remove and place the eggplant, zucchini and 8 of the pepper pieces aside. Place the remaining 2 peppers in a small bowl covered with plastic for 30 minutes, to loosen the skin. Remove and discard the skin and purée the peppers. Mix with the mayonnaise.

Spread the red pepper mayonnaise on half the bread slices. Top with eggplant, zucchini, peppers, tomatoes, arugula and fontina, dividing the ingredients equally among the 8 slices. Top with the remaining bread slices. Butter the outsides of the sandwiches.

In a sauté pan, cook the sandwiches over medium heat, turning once, until both sides of each sandwich are golden brown and the cheese has melted. (Lower the heat, if necessary, to prevent burning.)

I like this with a hearty Tuscan bread. If you want to cut down the fat, spread red pepper purée on the bread instead of mayo (increase the red peppers to 6, and add the extra pepper to the purée).

Ham and Swiss Sandwich

Makes 8 sandwiches

1/2	medium red onion, sliced	½
⅓ cup	grainy Dijon mustard	80 mL
16	slices marble rye bread	16
1½ lbs.	sliced ham	680 g
8	slices Swiss cheese	8

Grill or sauté the onion until light brown, about 6 minutes. Spread mustard on half the bread slices. Top each sandwich with sliced ham, one slice of Swiss cheese and 2–3 onion rings, then top with the remaining bread slices.

Butter the outsides of the sandwiches.

In a sauté pan, cook the sandwiches over medium heat, turning once, until both sides of each sandwich are golden brown and the cheese has melted. (Lower the heat, if necessary, to prevent burning.)

This classic sandwich gets a flavor boost from the grilled red onions, which add just a touch of sweetness.

Turkey, Grilled Pineapple and Arugula on Ciabatta

Makes 6 sandwiches

1	pineapple, peeled and cored	1
2	small loaves ciabatta or rustic Italian bread	2
4 Tbsp.	mayonnaise	60 mL
1½ lbs.	turkey breast, roasted and thinly sliced	680 g
2 cups	arugula	475 mL
	red pepper flakes (optional)	

Cut the pineapple into thin slices, about ¼ inch (.6 cm). Grill over high heat for about 1 minute per side.

Cut the loaves in half lengthwise.

Spread mayonnaise on the bottom halves of the ciabatta and top with sliced turkey. Top with grilled pineapple and arugula. Sprinkle with red pepper flakes, if desired, then cover with the top half of the ciabatta.

Slice each loaf crosswise into 3 sandwiches and arrange on a platter to serve.

Ciabatta, so called because of its slipper-like shape, is a dense bread made with olive oil. It may be made with herbs, caramelized onions, roasted garlic, or grated cheese, or simply baked plain.

"Gazpacho" Sandwich with Peppers, Cucumber and Red Onion

Makes 8 sandwiches

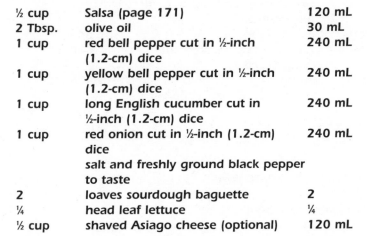

This sandwich tastes like summertime year round!

½ cup	Salsa (page 171)	120 mL
2 Tbsp.	olive oil	30 mL
1 cup	red bell pepper cut in ½-inch (1.2-cm) dice	240 mL
1 cup	yellow bell pepper cut in ½-inch (1.2-cm) dice	240 mL
1 cup	long English cucumber cut in ½-inch (1.2-cm) dice	240 mL
1 cup	red onion cut in ½-inch (1.2-cm) dice	240 mL
	salt and freshly ground black pepper to taste	
2	loaves sourdough baguette	2
¼	head leaf lettuce	¼
½ cup	shaved Asiago cheese (optional)	120 mL

Combine the salsa and olive oil and toss with the peppers, cucumber and red onion. Season with salt and pepper.

Cut the baguettes in half lengthwise. Line the bottom halves with leaf lettuce and top with the gazpacho salad. Add some shaved Asiago, if desired. Cover with the top halves of the baguettes and cut each loaf into 4 sandwiches.

Smoked Meat, Pickled Red Cabbage and Swiss Cheese on Pumpernickel Bagels

Makes 8

8	pumpernickel bagels	8
4 Tbsp.	mustard	60 mL
1 ½ lbs.	Montreal-style smoked meat, thinly sliced	680 g
2 cups	Pickled Red Cabbage	475 mL
8	slices Swiss cheese	8

Slice the bagels in half. Spread ½ Tbsp. (7.5 mL) mustard on the bottom half of each bagel. Top with smoked meat, pickled cabbage and Swiss cheese, and cover with the tops of the bagels.

Pickled Red Cabbage

½	head red cabbage	½
3 Tbsp.	vegetable oil	45 mL
	salt and freshly ground black pepper to taste	
⅓ – ½ cup	red wine vinegar	80–120 mL
5	juniper berries	5
¼ tsp.	caraway seeds	1.2 mL

Remove the core from the cabbage and slice the cabbage into thin strips. In a large pan over medium heat, sauté the cabbage in the vegetable oil for 10 minutes. Season with salt and pepper.

Add the red wine vinegar, juniper berries and caraway seeds. Cover and cook for about 30 minutes, until the cabbage is cooked through. Let cool. This pickled cabbage will keep in a glass jar in the fridge for about 2 weeks.

An excellent candidate for the picnic basket— one of the few sandwiches that can be made ahead without a loss in quality.

Pizza Dough

Makes 10 12-inch (30-cm) pizzas

½ oz.	fresh yeast, or 1½ oz. (42 mL) dried	13 g
2 Tbsp.	olive oil	30 mL
2 Tbsp.	honey	30 mL
2½ cups	warm water	600 mL
6–7 cups	flour	1.5–1.75 L
2 Tbsp.	salt	30 mL

At home I use a pizza stone to get a delicious crispy crust. I heat it in the oven for 5 minutes before putting the dough onto the stone. You can freeze any dough you don't want to use immediately for up to 2 months. Just wrap it in plastic wrap. Thaw before using.

Combine the yeast, olive oil, honey and warm water in a bowl and mix thoroughly. Let sit for 7–10 minutes. The mixture should foam slightly.

In a mixing bowl with a dough hook or paddle attachment, mix the flour and salt at low speed. Use a large bowl if making the dough by hand and mix well.

Slowly add the yeast mixture to the flour mixture on low speed. Keep mixing until the dough no longer sticks to the sides and the hook or paddle. Add more flour if it's sticky. If mixing by hand, use a wooden spoon to stir the yeast mixture into the flour. When a shaggy dough begins to form, turn it onto a floured surface and knead for about 10 minutes, until the dough is smooth and silky.

Remove the dough and place it in an oiled bowl. Cover with a damp towel and let sit at room temperature for 30 minutes, or until doubled in size.

Preheat the oven to 400°F (200°C). Transfer the dough to a floured surface. Divide it into 10 balls. Roll each ball out to form a 12-inch (30-cm) round, freezing any extras. Place on a pizza sheet or preheated pizza stone.

Bake the pizza dough until lightly browned, 4–5 minutes. Remove from the oven and add the desired toppings. Return to the oven for 20–25 minutes.

Four-Cheese Pizza with Artichoke Hearts and Cilantro Oil

Makes 1 12-inch (30-cm) pizza

1	pizza round, prebaked for 4–5 minutes (page 68)	1
¼ cup	chopped artichoke hearts	60 mL
¼ cup	grated fontina cheese	60 mL
¼ cup	grated mozzarella cheese	60 mL
¼ cup	grated white Cheddar cheese	60 mL
4	slices bocconcini	4
2 Tbsp.	Cilantro Oil (page 176)	30 mL

Preheat the oven to 400°F (200°C).

Spread the artichoke hearts and cheeses evenly over the prebaked pizza crust. Bake for approximately 20–25 minutes, until the cheese melts.

Drizzle cilantro oil over the pizza.

Smoked Chicken Pizza with Mozzarella, Onions and Barbecue Sauce

Makes 1 12-inch (30-cm) pizza

½	medium red onion, sliced into rings	½
¼ cup	Barbecue Sauce (page 174)	60 mL
1	pizza round, prebaked for 4–5 minutes (page 68)	1
½ cup	smoked chicken, cut into ½-inch (1.2-cm) dice	120 mL
¾ cup	grated mozzarella cheese	180 mL

Grill or sauté the onion rings for 2 minutes. Set aside.

Preheat the oven to 400°F (200°C). Spread barbecue sauce over the entire pizza round. Top with the smoked chicken, onions and cheese. Bake the pizza for approximately 20–25 minutes, until the cheese melts.

Give your guests an option: a vegetarian pizza generously topped with four types of cheese or a smoked chicken pizza with our not-too-sweet barbecue sauce. Most will want both.

Caramelized Onions and Chorizo Pizza with Fontina and Sun-dried Tomatoes

Makes 1 12-inch (30-cm) pizza

1	pizza round, prebaked for 4–5 minutes (page 68)	1
½ cup	Caramelized Onions (page 59)	120 mL
½ cup	sliced spicy chorizo	120 mL
¼ cup	sun-dried tomatoes, julienned	60 mL
¾ cup	grated fontina cheese	180 mL

Here's an updated "pepperoni" pizza, plus the one that Susan most often ate for lunch. When we added it to the bistro menu, it became Susan's Own.

Preheat the oven to 400°F (200°C). Spread caramelized onions evenly over the entire pizza round. Distribute the chorizo, sun-dried tomatoes and fontina over the onions.

Bake for approximately 20–25 minutes, until the cheese is bubbly.

Susan's Own Pizza

Makes 1 12-inch (30-cm) pizza

1	pizza round, prebaked for 4–5 minutes (page 68)	1
¼ cup	Caramelized Onions (page 59)	60 mL
½ cup	roasted yellow and red bell peppers, julienned (see Roasting Peppers, page 173)	120 mL
½ cup	sliced wild mushrooms (shiitake, oysters and portobellos)	120 mL
¾ cup	grated fontina cheese	180 mL

Preheat the oven to 400°F (200°C). Spread the caramelized onions evenly over the pizza round. Top with the peppers, mushrooms and fontina.

Bake for approximately 20–25 minutes, until the cheese melts.

Eggplant Pizza

Makes 1 12-inch (30-cm) pizza

½ cup	Japanese eggplant sliced into ¼-inch (.6-cm) rounds	120 mL
1 Tbsp.	olive oil	15 mL
1	pizza round, prebaked for 4–5 minutes (page 68)	1
½ cup	roasted yellow and red bell peppers, julienned (see Roasting Peppers, page 173)	120 mL
¾ cup	grated mozzarella cheese	180 mL
¼ cup	crumbled goat cheese	60 mL
2 Tbsp.	Basil Oil (page 176)	30 mL

Preheat the oven to 400°F (200°C). Toss the eggplant in the olive oil and place on a baking sheet. Roast for 5–7 minutes. Remove and spread with the other toppings evenly over the pizza round.

Bake for approximately 20–25 minutes, until the cheese melts. Drizzle with the basil oil.

The goat cheese in this pizza provides a slightly tart contrast to the rich sweetness of the roasted eggplant and peppers.

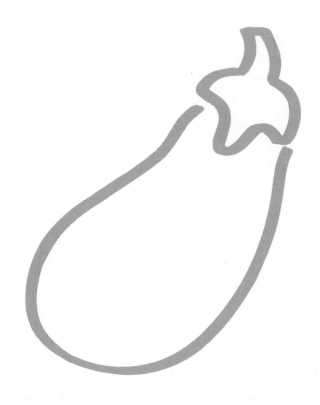

entrées: fish & seafood

Tuna "Pepper Steak" with Cucumber Salsa

Makes 8

4 Tbsp.	butter	60 mL
2 Tbsp.	minced shallots	30 mL
3 Tbsp.	white peppercorns	45 mL
3 Tbsp.	pink peppercorns	45 mL
2 Tbsp.	sherry	30 mL
2 Tbsp.	brandy	30 mL
1½ cups	whipping cream	360 mL
4 Tbsp.	Demi-glace (page 170)	60 mL
	salt to taste	
8	6-oz. (170-g) tuna steaks, at least ¾-inch (1.9-cm) thick	8
1 recipe	Cucumber Salsa	1 recipe

Just like a strip loin or New York steak that has been prepared *au poivre*, tuna attains another level when crusted with peppercorns before cooking. With tuna, we use white and pink peppercorns for a less spicy balance. A word of advice: sear the tuna steaks well and don't cook them past medium-rare to get the most delicious results.

To make the peppercorn sauce, melt half the butter in a sauté pan. Add the minced shallots and 1 Tbsp. (15 mL) each of the pink and white peppercorns. Cook on low heat until the shallots "sweat" and the peppercorns are fragrant, about 1 minute. Pour in the sherry and brandy and stir well. Add the whipping cream and demi-glace. Bring to a boil and reduce slightly. Remove from the heat. To finish, swirl in the remaining butter and season with salt. You can prepare this sauce ahead and reheat it when the tuna is ready.

Combine the remaining pink and white peppercorns. Place them on a hard surface or cutting board. Using the bottom of a sauté pan and with a rocking motion, crush the peppercorns. Set them aside on a plate.

Brush vegetable oil on both sides of the tuna steaks and press them into the crushed peppercorn blend. Reheat the peppercorn sauce if necessary.

Cook the steaks over medium-high heat in a sauté pan, about 2–2½ minutes per side. Season both sides with salt.

To serve, place the steaks on a platter and pour the peppercorn sauce over them. Serve the cucumber salsa on the side.

Cucumber Salsa

½ tsp.	red pepper flakes	2.5 mL
1 Tbsp.	vegetable oil	15 mL
2 Tbsp.	white wine vinegar	30 mL
2 tsp.	sugar	10 mL
1	long English cucumber, halved lengthwise, seeded and thinly sliced	1
½	red onion, diced	½

In a large bowl, combine the red pepper flakes, vegetable oil, white wine vinegar and sugar to make a dressing.

Blend thoroughly, then add the cucumber and onion and stir well.

Fettuccine with Salmon, Sea Bass, Mussels and Clams in Roasted Red Pepper Sauce

Serves 8

8	cloves garlic	8
5–6	red peppers, cored, seeded and quartered	5–6
1 cup	olive oil	240 mL
2 lbs.	fettuccine	900 g
1 lb.	mussels, cleaned	455 g
1 lb.	littleneck clams	455 g
¾ cup	white wine	180 mL
½ cup	whipping cream	120 mL
1½ lbs.	salmon, cut into ½-inch (1.2-cm) chunks	680 g
1½ lbs.	sea bass, cut into ½-inch (1.2-cm) chunks	680 g
	salt and freshly ground black pepper to taste	
	red pepper flakes	
	chopped fresh herbs (parsley, chives, rosemary and thyme)	

A combination greater than the sum of its parts. The sweetness of roasted peppers amplifies the flavor of both the finfish and shellfish.

Preheat the oven to 350°F (175°C). In a large bowl, toss the garlic cloves and red peppers with 1 Tbsp. (15 mL) of the olive oil. Place the peppers and garlic in a baking dish and roast in the oven for about 20 minutes, or until blisters appear on the skin of the peppers and the garlic has turned golden brown. Remove from the oven and set the garlic aside.

Place the peppers in a bowl covered with plastic wrap for a few minutes (this will allow the skin to separate more easily from the flesh). Peel the skins off the bell peppers. Set 4–5 quarters aside and put the rest in the bowl of a food processor or blender along with the roasted garlic and ½ cup (120 mL) of the olive oil. Purée and season with salt and black pepper. Cut the remaining peppers into julienne strips and set aside.

Cook the fettuccine in boiling salted water. Dried fettuccine will take about 8–9 minutes to cook *al dente*. When ready, drain in a colander and run cold water over the noodles to stop them from cooking any further. Drain and set aside.

Place the mussels and clams in a small pot or Dutch oven. Pour in the white wine and ¼ cup (60 mL) of the olive oil. Cover with a lid and cook over medium-high heat for 5 minutes, or until all the shellfish have steamed open. Discard any that do not open. Set aside in a warm place, covered.

In a large-bottomed pan over medium heat sauté the salmon and sea bass chunks in 3 Tbsp. (45 mL) of the olive oil. Add the shellfish with their juice, the roasted red pepper purée, julienned strips of pepper and whipping cream. Bring the sauce to a simmer, then gently stir in the fettuccine. Season with salt, black pepper and red pepper flakes.

To serve, mound the fettuccine in the center of a large platter, arrange the seafood on top of the pasta and garnish with chopped fresh herbs.

Couscous-Crusted Rock Cod with Iberian-style Garbanzo Bean Stew

Serves 8

2 cups	large-grain couscous	475 mL
2 Tbsp.	olive oil	30 mL
1 cup	onion, diced	240 mL
1	stalk celery, diced	1
1	carrot, diced	1
2 Tbsp.	minced garlic	30 mL
2	bay leaves	2
3	potatoes, peeled and diced	3
2 cups	Vegetable Stock (page 168)	475 mL
2 cups	garbanzo beans	475 mL
2 cups	tomato sauce	475 mL
	salt and freshly ground black pepper to taste	
1 Tbsp.	extra virgin olive oil	15 mL
8	6-oz. (170-g) rock cod fillets	8

A complex-sounding dish, but it is quite simple and full of down-to-earth flavors.

To cook the couscous, bring 4 cups (950 mL) of water to a boil. Add the couscous and cook for 10 minutes, or until the couscous is soft. Drain and set aside.

Heat the 2 Tbsp. (30 mL) olive oil over medium heat in a saucepan. Sauté the onion, celery and carrot with the garlic and bay leaves. Add the potatoes and vegetable stock. Cover the pan and bring the mixture to a boil, then simmer for about 10 minutes. Add the garbanzo beans and tomato sauce. If it's too thick, thin it out with more vegetable stock. Cook for another 12–15 minutes over medium-low heat, stirring occasionally, until the potatoes are cooked and the beans are tender. Season with salt and black pepper. Stir in the 1 Tbsp. (15 mL) of extra virgin olive oil. Set aside.

Preheat the oven to 375°F (190°C).

Season each cod fillet with salt and pepper, then brush with olive oil. On the top side of each fillet, apply a thin layer of couscous to form a crust. Place on a baking sheet and bake for about 10–12 minutes, until the fish flakes easily and is opaque.

Set out 8 pasta bowls and pour about ½ cup (120 mL) of garbanzo stew into each bowl. On top of the stew, place a crusted cod fillet.

Roast Salmon with Caramelized Onions and Balsamic Vinegar Compote

Serves 8

¼ cup	balsamic vinegar	60 mL
8	4-oz. (113-g) fillets salmon	8
4 Tbsp.	canola oil *olive oil)*	60 mL
½ cup	Caramelized Onions (page 59)	120 mL
½ cup	white wine	120 mL
2 Tbsp.	butter	30 mL
	salt and white pepper to taste	

Handwritten margin notes: 8 oz, 1 T, ¼ c led win, 1 T

In a small saucepan, bring the balsamic vinegar to a boil. Reduce until you have 2 Tbsp. (30 mL) left. Set aside.

Preheat the oven to 400°F (200°C).

Sear both sides of the salmon in a hot sauté pan with the oil, about 5 minutes. Transfer to a greased baking sheet. Bake until cooked through, approximately 10 minutes.

Drain the oil from the sauté pan and add the caramelized onions, white wine and reduced balsamic vinegar. Bring to a boil, turn down to a simmer and cook for about 5 minutes, stirring, until slightly reduced. Swirl in the butter and season with salt and white pepper.

To serve, place the salmon on a platter and pour the sauce over and around it.

The sweetness of caramelized onions blended with the light acidity of balsamic vinegar makes this sauce a perfect accompaniment for pan-roasted salmon. Serve with roasted potatoes and lots of crusty bread.

Halibut Parcels with Tomato Cilantro Sauce

Makes 8

⅔ cup	halved and seeded tomatoes (about 3 Roma tomatoes)	160 mL
6 Tbsp.	chopped cilantro	90 mL
2 Tbsp.	garlic	30 mL
1 Tbsp.	ginger	15 mL
4 Tbsp.	green onions	60 mL
1 Tbsp.	sesame oil	15 mL
8	4-oz. (113-g) halibut fillets	8
8	sheets rice paper, 10-inch (25-cm) rounds	8
2 Tbsp.	vegetable oil	30 mL
1 cup	white wine	240 mL
½ cup	Fish Stock (page 169)	120 mL
6 Tbsp.	butter	90 mL

Like the Vietnamese salad rolls, these "parcels" use rice paper, but these rice papers are larger and circular. This recipe was on our first bistro menu. We bring it back for occasional repeat performances.

Preheat the oven to 350°F (175°C). Place the tomatoes on a baking sheet and bake until they are dried, about 30–40 minutes. Cool and coarsely chop.

In a food processor or blender, mix the cilantro, garlic, ginger and green onion. Blend in the sesame oil until a paste is formed. Set aside 2 Tbsp. (30 mL) for the sauce.

Spread the paste evenly over one side of each piece of fish.

Working with one rice paper at a time, soak it for 15–20 seconds in warm water. Remove and place it on a clean surface. Place a piece of halibut on the center of the rice wrap. Fold the bottom, sides and top over to completely wrap the halibut.

In a very hot sauté pan with the oil, sear the parcels. Finish them in the oven for approximately 10 minutes, or until they are lightly browned.

In a sauté pan, sauté the 2 Tbsp. (30 mL) of reserved paste with the roasted tomatoes. Add the white wine and fish stock and bring to a boil. Reduce the heat and swirl in the butter.

To serve, place the parcels on a platter, and pour sauce over and around them.

Baked Sea Bass with Pistachio Crust and Orange Basil Sauce

Serves 8

5 cups	pistachios, coarsely ground	1.25 L
1 cup	dry bread crumbs	240 mL
6	egg whites, lightly beaten	6
8	4-oz. (113-g) sea bass fillets	8
	salt and freshly ground white pepper to taste	
4 Tbsp.	vegetable oil	60 mL
1 recipe	Orange Basil Sauce	1 recipe

Preheat the oven to 350° (175°C).

Mix the pistachios and bread crumbs on a plate. Place the egg whites in a shallow pan.

Season the sea bass with salt and white pepper. Dip one side of each fillet in egg white, then into the pistachio–bread crumb mixture to make a crust.

Heat the oil in a hot sauté pan, and sear the crusted side of the fillets. Place on a baking sheet and finish in the oven for 18–20 minutes or until the sea bass is flaky.

Serve the sea bass on a platter and drizzle the orange basil sauce over and around the fish.

Its natural oils prevent sea bass from drying out, and the green pistachios make a crispy crunchy crust with a beautiful hue.

Orange Basil Sauce

2 cups	orange juice	475 mL
1 cup	white wine	240 mL
2 Tbsp.	honey	30 mL
1 cup	whipping cream	240 mL
2 tsp.	chopped orange zest	10 mL
½ cup	orange segments	120 mL
	salt and black pepper to taste	
¼ cup	butter	60 mL
2 Tbsp.	chopped basil	30 mL

In a saucepan, combine the orange juice, white wine, honey and whipping cream. Bring to a boil, then reduce the heat and add the orange zest and segments. Season with salt and pepper. Continue to cook until it's reduced by about one-third. Remove from the heat, swirl in the butter and add the basil.

Linguine and Rice Noodles with Prawns in Thai Green Curry Sauce

Serves 8

1 lb.	linguine	455 g
1 lb.	rice noodles (mai fun)	455 g
2	Japanese eggplants, cut diagonally into ¼-inch (.6-cm) slices	2
1½	carrots, julienned	1½
1½	red peppers, julienned	1½
1	red onion, cut into thin slices	1
48	jumbo prawns, peeled and deveined	48
1 recipe	**Thai Green Curry Sauce**	1 recipe

The firmness of linguine combined with the smoothness of mai fun adds texture to this west coast version of a popular Thai curry, known as Keaw Wan Koong. You definitely have to go to an Asian food market to get the ingredients, but the effort is worth it.

Bring a large pot of salted water to a boil and cook the linguine for 7–8 minutes. Bring another pot of water to a boil and cook the rice noodles for 5 minutes. Drain both noodles, rinse under cold running water, drain and set aside.

In a wok, stir-fry the eggplant, carrots, red peppers and onion. Add the prawns and stir-fry until cooked, about 4 minutes. Remove the prawns to a plate, cover and keep warm.

Pour the Thai green curry sauce into the wok. Bring to a boil. Add the linguine and rice noodles and toss well.

To serve, place the noodles and vegetables on a platter in a large bowl. Arrange the prawns on top of the noodles.

Thai Green Curry Sauce

1	white onion, minced	1
1	knob galangal, minced (can be found in Asian markets)	1
1½ Tbsp.	minced garlic	22.5 mL
1 tsp.	shrimp paste	5 mL
2 Tbsp.	vegetable oil	30 mL
4	kaffir lime leaves, finely chopped	4
½ cup	Thai basil, tightly packed	120 mL
¼ cup	cilantro, tightly packed	60 mL
3 cups	coconut milk	720 mL
1 Tbsp.	fish sauce	15 mL
1 tsp.	chopped green chiles (optional)	5 mL

Sauté the onion, galangal, garlic and shrimp paste in vegetable oil. Stir in the kaffir lime leaves, Thai basil and cilantro. Pour in the coconut milk and bring to a boil. Simmer for about 5 minutes to reduce slightly. Stir in the fish sauce and chopped green chiles, if desired.

Asian Risotto with Shrimp and Scallops

Serves 10

6 Tbsp.	butter	90 mL
½ lb.	shiitake mushrooms, cut into strips	225 g
6	cloves garlic, minced	6
2 cups	Arborio rice	475 mL
6½ cups	chicken broth or vegetable stock	1.6 L
6 Tbsp.	sherry	90 mL
2 Tbsp.	soy sauce	30 mL
1 tsp.	chili sauce	5 mL
1	small red bell pepper, chopped	1
1 lb.	shrimp, deveined and split	455 g
½ lb.	scallops	225 g
½ cup	pine nuts	120 mL
1 cup	grated Parmesan cheese (Reggianno or Grana Padano)	240 mL

The better the quality of the cheese, the better the finished product. I always let my guests share in the stirring of the risotto. This way I'm not exhausted before the meal begins.

In a sauté pan, melt 2 Tbsp. (30 mL) of the butter. Add the shiitake mushrooms and sauté for 5 minutes. Set aside.

In a large pot, melt the remaining 4 Tbsp. (60 mL) of butter and sauté the ginger and garlic for a few seconds. Add the rice and cook for 3 minutes over medium heat.

Mix together the stock, sherry, soy sauce and chili sauce. Add the mixture, one-third at a time, to the sauté pan, stirring constantly until it is all absorbed. This takes about 20 minutes. Make sure to stir the rice continually.

Stir in the pepper, shrimps and scallops, and simmer for 4–5 minutes. Add the pine nuts and mushrooms and cook for 1 minute.

Stir in the grated cheese and serve immediately.

Swimming Scallops

Serves 4

2 tsp.	butter	10 mL
½	stalk lemon grass, thinly sliced	½
3	kaffir lime leaves, chopped (available in Asian stores)	3
1	knob galangal, chopped (available in Asian stores)	1
2	green onions, sliced	2
1 tsp.	sambal oelek	5 mL
1 cup	clam juice	240 mL
1 cup	coconut milk	240 mL
2½ lbs.	pink swimming scallops	1.1 kg
2 tsp.	chopped cilantro	10 mL

In a sauté pan, melt the butter and sauté the lemon grass, lime leaves, galangal, green onions and sambal oelek for 3 minutes, until softened.

Add the clam juice and coconut milk. Bring to a boil.

Toss in the scallops. Reduce the heat, cover and simmer for 10 minutes. To test for doneness, feel the scallops; they should be firm.

To serve, pile the scallops high in a bowl. Pour the sauce over and garnish with cilantro.

This dish is beautiful to look at. Try saving the shells—wash them well and keep them for decorating seafood platters.

entrées: meat

Roast Rack of Lamb with a Mushroom Crust

Makes 8

4 cups	mixed wild mushrooms (shiitake and oyster)	950 mL
3	minced shallots	3
2 Tbsp.	vegetable oil	30 mL
1 cup	fresh bread crumbs (from French or sourdough, crust removed)	240 mL
¼ cup	finely chopped fresh herbs (thyme, parsley, chives)	60 mL
½ cup	Rosemary Oil (page 175)	120 mL
2¼ cups	Dijon mustard	535 mL
8	racks of lamb, trimmed of fat and frenched (each portion should have 4–5 rib bones)	8
½ cup	diced onion	120 mL
½ cup	diced carrots	120 mL
¼ cup	diced celery	60 mL
2 tsp.	minced garlic	10 mL
2 Tbsp.	olive oil	30 mL
4 cups	cooked white beans	950 mL
1 Tbsp.	sherry vinegar	15 mL
	salt and black pepper to taste	

Rack of lamb is a great entrée for special occasions. For greater ease in preparation, order it "frenched" from your butcher. Frenching trims the meat, fat and gristle from the end of the bone to expose it for an attractive presentation.

Sauté the mushrooms and shallots in the vegetable oil over medium heat. Cook until the mushrooms have released most of their liquid.

Drain the mushrooms and shallots. Process in a food processor until minced. Cook the minced mixture over medium-high heat until almost all the moisture has evaporated. Set aside to cool.

Preheat the oven to 400°F (200°C).

In a mixing bowl, combine the bread crumbs, fresh herbs and mushrooms. Season to taste with salt and pepper and mix thoroughly.

Make a paste with ¼ cup (60 mL) rosemary oil and the Dijon mustard. Rub the paste on the fat cap of the racks. (If your racks were properly trimmed, there should be a thin layer of fat covering the meat. Most of this fat will melt away during cooking.) Press the mushroom mix onto the racks.

Put the racks on a baking sheet and roast to your desired degree of doneness. Medium-rare will take 18–20 minutes.

While the lamb cooks, sauté the onion, carrots, celery and garlic in 1 Tbsp. (15 mL) of the olive oil over medium heat until soft. Add the beans and 2 cups (475 mL) of water. Heat through and stir in the sherry vinegar and the remaining 1 Tbsp. (15 mL) olive oil. Season with salt and pepper.

To serve, mound the bean mixture in the center of a large platter. Surround it with the racks. Drizzle the remaining rosemary oil over the racks.

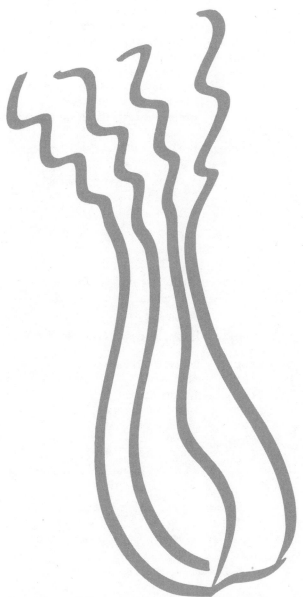

Beef Tenderloin and Asian Noodles

Serves 8

4 Tbsp.	vegetable oil	60 mL
6–7 oz.	tenderloin, cut into thin strips	170–200 g
2	medium red onions, cut into thin strips	2
½	head napa cabbage, cut into thin strips	½
2	medium red bell peppers, cut into thin strips	2
1 lb.	snow peas, cut into strips	455 g
1 recipe	Black Bean Hoisin Sauce	1 recipe
2 Tbsp.	sesame oil	30 mL
8 cups	cooked Shanghai noodles (available in the refrigerated case of Asian supermarkets)	2 L
2	green onions, sliced on a diagonal	2

If you're serving meat eaters and vegetarians, it's easy to cook the meat separately and have two dishes that will please everyone.

Heat the oil in a very hot wok. Stir-fry the tenderloin for 5 minutes.

Add the onion, cabbage, red pepper and snow peas. Stir-fry for 1 minute.

Add the Black Bean Hoisin Sauce, sesame oil and Shanghai noodles. Bring the sauce to a boil.

To serve, pile high in a pasta bowl. Garnish with green onions.

Black Bean Hoisin Sauce

½ cup	black bean sauce	120 mL
½ cup	soy sauce	120 mL
½ cup	hoisin sauce	120 mL
¼ cup	balsamic vinegar	60 mL
¼ cup	sesame oil	60 mL
2 Tbsp.	sugar	30 mL

Thoroughly combine all the ingredients by hand.

Grilled Tenderloin with Wilted Peppery Greens and Cabernet Demi-glace

Serves 8

8	tenderloin steaks	8
1 Tbsp.	canola oil	15 mL
2 cups	Demi-glace (page 170)	475 mL
¼ cup	Cabernet or any full-bodied red wine	60 mL
4 Tbsp.	butter	60 mL
2 cups	arugula	475 mL
2 cups	watercress	475 mL
	salt and freshly ground black pepper to taste	
	vegetable oil	

Brush the steaks with a little oil and season with freshly ground pepper. Set them aside while you preheat your barbecue.

Place the steaks on the hot grill and cook to your preference. (When serving a crowd, we cook all our steaks to medium.)

While the steaks are cooking, combine the demi-glace and wine in a saucepan over medium heat and bring to a simmer for 3 minutes. Remove the pan from the heat, and stir the butter into the sauce.

In a sauté pan over medium heat, heat the oil. Add the watercress and arugula alternately by the handful. Add about 4 Tbsp. (60 mL) water and cover the pan. Cook for a minute or so to wilt the greens. Season with salt and pepper to taste. Set aside and keep warm.

To serve, lay the wilted greens on a platter. Top with the steaks. Serve with the sauce on the side.

Sophisticated as the name might suggest it is, this is actually an easy way to dress up a tenderloin steak or filet mignon prepared on the barbecue. You can cook the steaks on the stovetop in a heavy sauté pan, if you prefer not to use the barbecue.

Rib-Eye Steak with Roasted Garlic Butter

Serves 8

8	9-oz. (255-g) rib-eye steaks	8
15	cloves garlic	15
½ cup	sherry	120 mL
1 Tbsp.	chopped thyme	15 mL
1 cup	butter, softened	240 mL
1 tsp.	chopped parsley	5 mL
1 tsp.	chopped chives	5 mL
	salt and freshly ground black pepper to taste	

This garlic butter will enhance any grilled food. Just keep it frozen and slice off rounds as needed.

Preheat the oven to 375°F (190°C). Coat the garlic cloves with some vegetable oil and roast in the oven till golden brown, about 12–15 minutes. Set aside.

In a small saucepan, combine the sherry and thyme and bring to a boil. Boil until the volume is reduced by half. Strain and discard the thyme.

Mince the roasted garlic and blend it with the butter in a bowl. Add the sherry and chopped herbs. Season with salt and pepper.

Lay a piece of clear plastic wrap on your work surface. Drop the butter mix on the wrap and roll it into a log. Freeze until ready to use.

When you're ready to grill the steaks, remove the butter from the freezer to soften slightly. Dredge the steaks in a little vegetable oil. Season with salt and pepper. Grill the steaks to the desired level of doneness, about 10 minutes for medium-rare, turning once.

To serve, arrange the steaks on a platter. Slice rounds of roasted garlic butter from the log and place them on top of the steaks. The heat of the steaks will melt the butter.

Brisket with Horseradish Cream

Serves 8

5 lbs.	beef brisket	2.25 kg
2 cups	onions, coarsely chopped	475 mL
2 cups	carrots, coarsely chopped	475 mL
2 cups	celery, coarsely chopped	475 mL
3–4 cups	beef stock	720–950 mL
2 cups	carrots, cut on the diagonal	475 mL
2 cups	green beans, cut on the diagonal	475 mL
2 Tbsp.	thyme	30 mL
	salt and black pepper to taste	
1 recipe	Horseradish Cream	1 recipe

Preheat the oven to 375°F (190°C). Heat a roasting pan over high heat on the stovetop, and brown the chopped onion, carrots and celery in a little oil. Set aside.

In a large, very hot sauté pan, brown both sides of the brisket. Place in the roasting pan with the browned vegetables. Add the beef stock to halfway cover the brisket and cover the pan with aluminum foil.

Bake for about 1½ hours, then flip the brisket. Add more stock and cook for another 45 minutes to 1 hour, until tender.

Remove the brisket from the oven and set it on a plate. Strain the juice and reserve; discard the vegetables. Allow the brisket to cool for 10–15 minutes.

Add the diagonally cut carrots, green beans and thyme to the roasting pan with reserved juice. Cover with foil and return to the oven for 20 minutes, or until the vegetables are tender.

Slice the brisket. Serve with the green beans, carrots, pan juices and horseradish cream.

This is a melt-in-your-mouth brisket that can be served for a leisurely lunch.

Horseradish Cream

1	Granny Smith apple, grated	1
2 cups	sour cream	475 mL
½	lemon, juice only	½
	salt and white pepper to taste	
1 Tbsp.	prepared horseradish	15 mL

Thoroughly combine all ingredients.

Bourgignon

5/27/05 - lots of work - ? worth it? mushroom compote good!

Serves 8

1½ cups	red wine *3/4*	360 mL
½ cup	vegetable oil *1/4*	120 mL
½	onion, chopped	½
5–6	black peppercorns *3*	5–6
2	bay leaves *1*	2
1 tsp.	minced garlic *½*	5 mL
2½ lbs.	beef, top round, cut into ¾-inch (1.9-cm) cubes *1½*	1.1 kg
2 Tbsp.	vegetable oil *1*	30 mL
1 cup	minced onion *½*	240 mL
½ cup	minced carrots *¼*	120 mL
½ cup	minced celery *¼*	120 mL
2 cups	red wine *1*	475 mL
3 cups	Demi-glace (page 170) *1½*	720 mL
3 cups	pearl onions, peeled *1½ c*	720 mL
1 Tbsp.	butter *1*	15 mL
2 tsp.	brown sugar *1*	10 mL
2 Tbsp.	chopped mixed herbs (Italian parsley, thyme and chives) *1*	30 mL
1 recipe	Wild Mushroom Compote salt and freshly ground black pepper to taste	1 recipe

This traditional French favorite has been updated with the addition of a wild mushroom compote flavored with balsamic vinegar.

To make a braising marinade, combine the red wine, ½ cup (120 mL) of oil, chopped onion, peppercorns, bay leaves and garlic. Let stand for an hour or so before using. Soak the cubed beef in the marinade overnight, in a covered dish in the fridge. Drain the beef and discard the marinade.

Preheat the oven to 325°F (165°C).

Heat the vegetable oil over medium heat in a large-bottomed ovenproof pan and sauté the minced onions, carrots and celery until the onions are translucent. Add the beef and brown on all sides. Season with salt and pepper.

Pour in the 2 cups (475 mL) red wine and the demi-glace. Bring to a simmer.

Cover the pan with a lid and braise slowly in the oven for about 1½–2 hours, until the meat can be flaked with a fork.

In a sauté pan over medium heat, heat the pearl onions with the butter. Stir in the brown sugar and cook until the onions are golden brown, about 4 minutes.

Add the pearl onions and chopped herbs to the beef pan. Season to taste with salt and pepper.

To serve, place in a serving dish and garnish with the wild mushroom compote.

Wild Mushroom Compote

2	chopped shallots	2
1 tsp.	butter	5 mL
1 tsp.	vegetable oil	5 mL
1½ cups	shiitake and portobello mushrooms	360 mL
	salt and freshly ground black pepper to taste	
1 Tbsp.	balsamic vinegar	15 mL
1 Tbsp.	fresh chopped herbs (rosemary, chives, thyme)	15 mL

Sauté the shallots in the butter and oil over medium-high heat.

Add the shiitake and portobello mushrooms. Season with salt and black pepper. Pour in the balsamic vinegar. Stir thoroughly. Blend in the chopped herbs.

Southwestern Shepherd's Pie

Serves 8 to 10

3 lbs.	lean ground beef	1.4 kg
2	onions, diced	2
2 Tbsp.	vegetable oil	30 mL
2	green bell peppers, diced	2
2 tsp.	chili powder	10 mL
¼ tsp.	cayenne pepper	1.2 mL
½ tsp.	ground cumin	2.5 mL
½ cup	chopped cilantro	120 mL
6	russet potatoes	6
½ cup	butter	120 mL
½ cup	whipping cream	120 mL
1 Tbsp.	smoked chipotle peppers in adobo, minced	15 mL
	salt and freshly ground white pepper to taste	
½ cup	sliced green onions	120 mL
	Parmesan cheese, grated	

Easy to make and a crowd pleaser to boot, this is reason enough to get together with your friends.

In a large-bottomed pan, sauté the ground beef and onions in the vegetable oil until browned. Add the green peppers, chili, cayenne and cumin. Season lightly with salt and white pepper. Cook for 5 minutes, then mix in the chopped cilantro. Drain in a colander and set aside.

While the beef mixture is cooking, put the potatoes in a soup pot and cover with water. Cook over medium heat until a knife slides through a potato easily, about 25 minutes. Drain and cool slightly. Peel the potatoes while still warm. Mash them with the butter, whipping cream and chipotle peppers. Season to taste with salt and white pepper. Mix in the green onions.

Preheat the oven to 350°F (175°C).

To assemble, oil the bottom of a 9- x 13-inch (23- x 33-cm) dish. Spread the ground beef mixture in the dish, layer the mashed potatoes over the beef and sprinkle grated Parmesan cheese on the mashed potatoes.

Bake for 35–40 minutes. Serve straight from the baking dish.

Roast Rack of Lamb with a Mushroom Crust (page 88)

Beef Tenderloin with Asian Noodles (page 90)

Chicken Chop with Sweet Onions, Peppers, Tomatoes and Olives (page 100)

entrées:
poultry

Pasta Paella with Smoked Chicken, Chorizo, Cod, Shellfish and Roasted Peppers

Serves 8

4 cups	chicken stock	950 mL
½ tsp.	saffron threads	2.5 mL
6 cups	orzo	1.5 L
3 Tbsp.	olive oil	45 mL
2 tsp.	minced garlic	10 mL
½ cup	diced onion	120 mL
8 oz.	ling cod, cut in 1-inch (2.5-cm) cubes	225 g
12 oz.	smoked chicken breast, julienned	340 g
6 oz.	spicy chorizo sausage, sliced	170 g
8 oz.	prawns, peeled and deveined	225 g
1 lb.	mussels, bearded and cleaned	475 g
¼ cup	white wine	60 mL
4	roasted red peppers (see Roasting Peppers, page 173), cut into strips	4
¼ cup	whipping cream salt and freshly ground black pepper to taste	60 mL
2 Tbsp.	chopped Italian or flat-leafed parsley	30 mL

In a pot, bring the chicken stock to a boil and remove from the heat. Make a "tea" by steeping the saffron in the chicken stock. Set aside.

In a large pot, bring 8 cups (2 L) of water to a boil, season with salt and pour in about 1 Tbsp. (15 mL) of oil. Add the orzo and cook till *al dente*, about 8 minutes. Drain and rinse under cold water. Set aside.

Pour the olive oil into a large-bottomed pot over medium heat. Lightly sauté the garlic and onion, then add the ling cod. Cook until the fish is seared on all sides, about 5 minutes.

Add the smoked chicken, chorizo, prawns and mussels, and cook for 3 minutes.

Pour in the white wine and scrape the bottom lightly to pick up the browned bits. This technique is called deglazing and it results in a more flavorful final product.

Cooked and served in a special pan, called a paellera, the sight of the pan laden with orange-colored rice and topped with meats and seafood is a showstopper. Our version uses orzo instead of the traditional rice, making it a touch lighter.

Remove the prawns to a dish. Set aside and keep warm.

Add the orzo and pour in the saffron tea.

Stir and cook till all the mussels have opened and the orzo is heated through, about another 5 minutes. Discard any mussels that are not opened.

Add the roasted peppers and whipping cream. Stir and season with salt and pepper.

Mound the orzo in the center of a large platter and arrange the meats, prawns and other seafood over and around the orzo. Sprinkle with chopped parsley.

Chicken Chop with Sweet Onions, Peppers, Tomatoes and Olives

Serves 8

8	chicken breasts, halved, with wing joint on	8
1 Tbsp.	olive oil	15 mL
½	medium onion, sliced thinly	½
½ cup	white wine	120 mL
2	medium tomatoes, roughly chopped	2
2	red or yellow bell peppers, julienned	2
	oregano to taste	
½ cup	black olives, washed and halved lengthwise	120 mL

Preheat the oven to 375°F (190°C).

Cut the tip off each "drumette" or wing joint. With a boning knife, push the meat on the bone toward the breast, thereby exposing the bone. This is a "frenching" technique that makes for an elegant presentation.

In a sauté pan, sear the chicken breast skin-side down in the oil. Place on a baking sheet and finish cooking in the oven for 16 minutes, or until cooked thoroughly. Pat with paper towels. Arrange on 8 plates and keep warm.

Drain the oil from the sauté pan, leaving 2 tsp. (10 mL). Add the onion and brown over low-medium heat, about 6–7 minutes. Add the white wine. Cook for 30 seconds. Add the tomatoes, peppers and oregano, turn up the heat and simmer for 2 minutes.

Add the olives. Pour the sauce over the chicken and serve immediately.

This is a simple-to-make bistro specialty that is easily translated for home use. It's great served on a bed of mashed potatoes.

Smoked Chicken Fettuccine with Portobello Mushrooms and Roasted Garlic

Serves 8

15	cloves garlic	15
¼ cup	vegetable oil	60 mL
4	whole portobello mushrooms, grilled and sliced	4
2 cups	smoked chicken, cubed	475 mL
½ cup	Caramelized Onions (page 59)	120 mL
12 cups	cooked fettuccine	3 L
¼ cup	chopped mixed herbs (rosemary, basil, thyme and oregano)	60 mL

"Roast" the garlic on the stovetop by cooking it in the ¼ cup (60 mL) oil for about 15–20 minutes. Remove the garlic from the oil and mince it.

Remove all but 2 Tbsp. (30 mL) of the sautéeing oil and sauté the minced garlic over high heat for 1 minute. Add the portobello mushrooms and chicken. Cook over medium heat for 3 minutes.

Toss in the caramelized onions, fettuccine and mixed herbs.

To serve, pile high in a pasta bowl.

This rich and flavorful dish is surprisingly low in fat.

Coconut Curry Chicken with Spicy Spinach and Tomato Ginger Sauce

Serves 8

8	tomatoes, halved and seeded	8
12	4-oz. (113-g) assorted chicken pieces with skin and bones (boneless skinless chicken can be also be used)	12
2	medium onions, chopped	2
1 Tbsp.	grated ginger	15 mL
2	cloves garlic, minced	2
4 Tbsp.	curry powder	60 mL
3 cups	coconut milk	720 mL
1 Tbsp.	oil	15 mL
1 cup	spinach	240 mL
½ Tbsp.	sambal oelek	7.5 mL
	salt and freshly ground black pepper to taste	

This is a full meal when the chicken is served with a platter of basmati rice.

Preheat the oven to 350°F (175°C). Place the tomatoes on a baking sheet and bake until they are dried, about 30–40 minutes. Cool and coarsely chop.

In a skillet over medium-high heat, brown the chicken pieces and half the chopped onion.

Add the roasted tomatoes, ginger, garlic, 2 Tbsp. (30 mL) of the curry powder and 1½ cups (360 mL) of the coconut milk. Bring to a boil. Simmer until the chicken is cooked, about 20 minutes.

Remove the chicken to a serving platter and keep warm. With a hand blender, purée the tomato sauce and keep it warm.

In a saucepan, heat 1 Tbsp. (15 mL) oil. Sauté the remaining chopped onion until translucent. Add the spinach, sambal oelek and remaining curry powder. Cook for 2 minutes. Add the remaining coconut milk. Bring to a boil. Taste and season with salt and pepper. Purée with a hand blender.

To serve, pour the tomato sauce over the chicken pieces. Drizzle the spinach sauce over everything.

Turkey Pasta Swirl with Pesto Alfredo

Serves 8

1½ lbs.	turkey, ground	680 g
½	onion, diced	½
1 Tbsp.	minced garlic	15 mL
2 Tbsp.	vegetable oil	30 mL
	salt and freshly ground white pepper to taste	
1½ lbs.	ricotta cheese	680 g
1 cup	grated mozzarella cheese	240 mL
⅔ cup	grated Parmesan cheese	160 mL
2	eggs	2
2 Tbsp.	fresh chopped basil	30 mL
2	lasagna sheets, 10 x 12 inches (25 x 30 cm)	2
2 cups	whipping cream	475 mL
⅔ cup	Pesto (page 171)	160 mL

Sauté the turkey, onion and garlic in vegetable oil over medium heat. Season with salt and white pepper. When cooked, about 10–12 minutes, set aside to cool. In a mixing bowl, thoroughly combine the ricotta, mozzarella, Parmesan, eggs and basil. Fold in the cooked turkey mixture and season to taste with salt and pepper.

Lay the cooked, thawed pasta sheets on the counter, with the shorter edge facing you. Spread the turkey-cheese mixture over the sheets, leaving about 1 inch (2.5 cm) of the far edge clear. Roll the filled sheets up tightly, jelly-roll style. Cut each roll into 8 equal slices.

Preheat the oven to 375°F (190°C).

Heat the whipping cream in a saucepan over medium heat. Simmer slowly for 10–15 minutes, or until the cream starts to thicken. Remove from the heat and stir in the pesto.

To assemble, grease the bottom of two 9- x 13-inch (23- x 33-cm) lasagna pans. Spread ¼ cup (60 mL) pesto sauce on the bottom of each dish. Lay 8 pasta swirls in each dish, cut side up, and pour the remaining pesto over each swirl.

Bake for 20–25 minutes, until brown on top.

This is one of those dishes that look like someone labored long and hard in the kitchen. But that is not the case here and it's delicious too. Lasagna sheets are normally sold cooked in the frozen section of your supermarket, or fresh sheets may be found in the fresh pasta case. This recipe can also be made with dry lasagna noodles. Cook 8 dried noodles in boiling salted water till tender, about 7–8 minutes, then drain. Follow the directions for rolling the lasagna sheets, but cut each noodle roll into 2 slices instead of 8.

entrées:
vegetarian

Spinach and Mushroom Cannelloni

Serves 8

3 cups	sliced shiitake mushrooms	720 mL
2 cups	sliced oyster mushrooms	475 mL
4 Tbsp.	vegetable oil	60 mL
5 cups	chopped spinach	1.25 L
	salt and freshly ground white pepper to taste	
2 lbs.	ricotta cheese	900 g
3	eggs	3
2 Tbsp.	minced garlic	30 mL
1½ cups	grated mozzarella cheese	360 mL
1 cup	grated Parmesan cheese	240 mL
3 Tbsp.	freshly chopped basil	45 mL
4	lasagna sheets, 10 x 12 inches (25 x 30 cm)	4
2 Tbsp.	minced garlic	30 mL
1 Tbsp.	butter	15 mL
2 cups	whipping cream	475 mL
2 cups	half-and-half cream	475 mL
1 cup	Parmesan cheese	240 mL
1 recipe	Tomato Sauce	1 recipe

This is a very easy dish to prepare. It is also a good dish to whip up when you've got lots of company coming. (See the introduction to Turkey Pasta Swirl, page 103, for information about lasagna sheets.)

Sauté the sliced mushrooms in vegetable oil over medium heat until lightly browned, about 3 minutes. Add the spinach and cook until just wilted. Season with salt and white pepper.

In a mixing bowl, combine the ricotta cheese, eggs, 2 Tbsp. (30 mL) garlic, mozzarella, 1 cup (240 mL) Parmesan cheese, basil and spinach-mushroom mixture. Mix well with your hands until thoroughly blended.

Cut each lasagna sheet into 4 equal rectangles. Arrange the rectangles on the counter so that the longer edge faces you. Fill a pastry bag with the stuffing and pipe the mixture along the front edge of the pasta rectangle. Continue this with the 16 rectangles, then roll the pasta around the stuffing away from you. You will now have 16 cannelloni.

Preheat the oven to 350°F (175°C).

To make the alfredo sauce, sauté the remaining 2 Tbsp. (30 mL) minced garlic with the butter for 1 minute. Stir in both creams and cook until the sauce is reduced by about one-quarter and is slightly thickened. Mix in the remaining 1 cup (240 mL) Parmesan cheese and season to taste with salt and pepper.

Pour the tomato sauce into a large baking dish. Arrange the cannelloni, seam side down, on the sauce. Pour the alfredo sauce over the cannelloni. Top with grated Parmesan cheese. Cover with aluminum foil and bake for 40–45 minutes. Remove the foil and bake for another 10–15 minutes, until the cheese melts.

Tomato Sauce

3	small onions, thinly sliced	3
2 Tbsp.	minced garlic	30 mL
1 Tbsp.	olive oil	15 mL
4	14-oz. (398-mL) cans whole Roma tomatoes	4
	salt and freshly ground black pepper to taste	

In a soup pot over medium-low heat, cook the onion and garlic in the olive oil until they are brown. Add the tomatoes. Cook until slightly thickened, about 25–30 minutes. Season with salt and black pepper. Purée with a hand blender or in a food processor.

Linguine with Caramelized Onions and Leeks in a Sun-dried Tomato Marinara

Serves 8

12 cups	cooked linguine	3 L
2 cups	sun-dried tomatoes	475 mL
2 Tbsp.	olive oil	30 mL
2 Tbsp.	minced garlic	30 mL
½	medium onion, diced	½
2 cups	crushed tomatoes	475 mL
1 cup	chopped leeks	240 mL
1 cup	Caramelized Onions (page 59)	240 mL
	salt and freshly ground black pepper to taste	

Caramelized onions are our trademark at the Lazy Gourmet. They add a sweet flavor to this pasta. For those non-vegetarians, you can add chicken or any meaty fish such as tuna or swordfish.

In a deep bowl, soak the sun-dried tomatoes in hot water for 6 minutes. Drain and chop. Set aside.

In a saucepan, heat 1 Tbsp. (15 mL) of the olive oil over medium-high heat. Sauté the garlic and diced onion for about 3 minutes, or until lightly brown. Add the crushed tomatoes and cook for approximately 10 minutes. Add the sun-dried tomatoes. Using a hand blender or blender, purée until smooth. Return to the saucepan and keep warm over low heat.

In a sauté pan, heat the remaining 1 Tbsp. (15 mL) olive oil. Sauté the leeks and caramelized onions for about 2 minutes.

Add the tomato sauce to the leek mixture and bring to a boil. Season to taste with salt and pepper. Toss in the hot linguine and serve immediately.

Mushroom Risotto with Olives, Green Beans and Grana Padano

Serves 4

¼ cup	butter	60 mL
3	cloves garlic, minced	3
2	medium white onions, finely diced	2
4 cups	rice	950 mL
½ cup	white wine	120 mL
8 cups	vegetable stock	2 L
2 Tbsp.	butter	30 mL
2 cups	mixed wild mushrooms (portobello, shiitake, oyster), sliced	480 mL
2 cups	green beans, trimmed of stringy ends and cut diagonally into 2-inch (5-cm) pieces	475 mL
¾ cup	kalamata olives, pitted, halved and rinsed	180 mL
½ lb.	Grana Padano cheese, shaved salt and freshly ground white pepper to taste	225 g

This risotto is comforting and satisfying. Adding smoked chicken will further enhance this beautiful dish.

In a large pot over medium heat, melt ¼ cup (60 mL) butter and sauté the garlic and onion until translucent. Add the rice and mix well. Stir in the white wine. Add just enough stock to cover the rice. Continue stirring so that the rice does not stick.

In a separate pan, sauté the mushrooms with 2 Tbsp. (30 mL) butter until they are slightly colored. Stir the mushrooms into the rice. Keep adding the stock to cover, stirring continuously, until the stock is used up and the rice is cooked.

Bring a pot of salted water to a boil and add the beans. Simmer for 6 minutes, or until tender, then quickly strain and run under cold running water.

Mix the beans and olives with the risotto. Season with salt and pepper.

To serve, place the risotto on a large platter and shave the Grana Padano over the top.

Mee Goreng

Serves 8

3 Tbsp.	vegetable oil	45 mL
1½ lbs.	snow peas, cut into strips	680 g
2	medium red bell peppers, cut into strips	2
½	head napa cabbage, cut into strips	½
1 cup	firm tofu, deep fried and cut in strips	240 mL
3 lbs.	cooked Shanghai noodles (available in the refrigerated section of Asian markets)	1.4 kg
½ cup	ketjap manis (sweet soy sauce, available in the Asian section of supermarkets)	120 mL
½ cup	sweet chili sauce (preferably Yeo brand)	120 mL
3 cups	bean sprouts	750 mL
½ cup	sliced green onions	120 mL

Could it be any easier? I didn't know that this complex-tasting dish could be so simple to prepare!

Heat a wok over high heat with the oil. Sauté the snow peas, red pepper, napa cabbage and tofu for 2 minutes.

Add the Shanghai noodles and ¼ cup (60 mL) of water. Stir-fry for 4 minutes.

Add the ketjap manis and sweet chili sauce. Bring the sauce to a boil. Add the bean sprouts and stir-fry for 1 minute.

Mound high in a pasta bowl and garnish with the green onions and fried shallots.

Fried Shallots

8	medium shallots, peeled and sliced	8
½ cup	all-purpose flour	120 mL
½ cup	vegetable oil	120 mL

Dredge the shallots in flour. Heat the oil and deep-fry the shallots until golden brown and crispy, or until the shallots are floating. Drain on paper towels.

Eggplant Moussaka

Serves 8

3	Italian eggplants, peeled and sliced	3
1½ cups	all-purpose flour	360 mL
6	eggs, beaten	6
2½ cups	canola oil	600 mL
½ cup	olive oil	120 mL
1 Tbsp.	olive oil	15 mL
2	medium onions, coarsely chopped	2
4–5	cloves garlic, minced	4–5
10	tomatoes, seeded and coarsely chopped	10
3 cups	Vegetable Stock (page 168)	720 mL
1 Tbsp.	honey	15 mL
1 Tbsp.	balsamic vinegar	15 mL
½ cup	shredded fontina cheese	120 mL
½ cup	shredded mozzarella cheese	120 mL
1 cup	grated Romano cheese	240 mL
1 cup	bread crumbs	240 mL

This is a great dish to make ahead and keep in the freezer for those nights when a large group comes over unexpectedly.

Dredge the eggplant in the flour, then dip in the beaten eggs.

Heat the canola oil and ½ cup (120 mL) olive oil in a Dutch oven or deep sauté pan to very hot, 350°F (175°C). (It must be hot or the eggplant becomes greasy.) Pan-fry the eggplant slices a few at a time, until golden brown. Drain on paper towel and set aside.

In a large saucepan, heat the 1 Tbsp. (15 mL) olive oil and sauté the onions and garlic until brown. Add the tomatoes and cook for 5 minutes. Add the vegetable stock, honey and balsamic vinegar. Bring to a boil and simmer for 10 minutes. Using a hand blender, purée the sauce.

Mix all the cheeses together and set aside.

Preheat the oven to 350°F (175°C).

In a 9- x 13-inch (23- x 33-cm) glass baking dish, place a layer of eggplant, a layer of tomato sauce, and a layer of cheese. Repeat, ending with a third layer of eggplant. Sprinkle the bread crumbs on top.

Bake for 30–40 minutes, until the cheese is melted and the bread crumbs are browned.

Gado-Gado Platter

Serves 8

1 bag	dry vermicelli noodles	1 bag
1	head broccoli, cut into florets	1
1	head cauliflower, cut into florets	1
2	medium carrots, cut into spears 2 inches (5 cm) long	2
3 lbs.	snow peas, trimmed	1.4 kg
4 tsp.	sesame oil	20 mL
2 Tbsp.	vegetable oil	30 mL
1	small red onion, cut into ½-inch-thick (1.2-cm) slices	1
1 tsp.	vegetable oil green leaf lettuce	5 mL
6–7	cherry tomatoes, halved	6–7
2 cups	mung bean sprouts	475 mL
1	small cucumber, cut diagonally into ½-inch (1.2-cm) slices	1
1 recipe	Fried Shallots (page 110)	1 recipe
1 recipe	Peanut Sauce (page 172)	1 recipe

This dish can be the spectacular showpiece of a summer buffet. Gado-gado is actually a mosaic of the different cultural influences on Indonesia. The Chinese noodles and Asian and European vegetables are flavored with locally inspired peanut sauce.

In a large pot, bring 4¼ cups (1 L) of water to a boil. Break apart the vermicelli noodles, add them to the boiling water, and cook for 5 minutes. Drain and run cold water over them. Drain and set aside.

Blanch the vegetables separately, the broccoli for 4 minutes, cauliflower for 4 minutes, carrots for 3 minutes and snow peas for 2 minutes. Drain and plunge into ice water. Drain well, place in individual bowls and toss each vegetable with a mixture of 1 tsp. (5 mL) sesame oil and ½ Tbsp. (7.5 mL) vegetable oil. Keeping the vegetables separate, set them aside.

In a sauté pan sauté the onions for 1 minute with the remaining 1 tsp. (5 mL) of vegetable oil. Set aside.

Line a large platter with green leaf lettuce and spread the vermicelli noodles over the entire platter. Arrange the broccoli, cauliflower, carrots, snow peas, onions, cherry tomatoes, bean sprouts and cucumber attractively on the vermicelli. Garnish with fried shallots and serve with peanut sauce.

side dishes

Seasonal Vegetables Roasted with Herb Butter

Serves 8

½ cup	cauliflower florets, separated	120 mL
1 cup	broccoli florets, separated	240 mL
2 cups	bell peppers (red, orange or yellow), cut into ½-inch (1.2-cm) strips	475 mL
1½ cups	asparagus	360 mL
1½ cups	carrots, cut diagonally into ½-inch (1.2-cm) slices	360 mL
1 cup	sliced portobello mushrooms, gills removed	240 mL
1½ cups	zucchini, cut diagonally into ½-inch (1.2-cm) slices	360 mL
2 Tbsp.	olive oil	30 mL
½ log	**Herb Butter**	**½ log**
	salt and freshly ground black pepper to taste	

Excellent for accompanying spring and summer dinners.

Blanch the cauliflower, broccoli, peppers, asparagus and carrots separately in boiling salted water for 1–3 minutes each. Drain. Refresh in ice water, then drain and set aside.

Sauté the portobello mushrooms and zucchini separately in the oil. Drain and set aside.

Preheat the oven to 450°F (230°C).

Pull a log of herb butter from the freezer and cut it in half. Replace the other half for future use. Cut the half log into thin disks. Toss all the vegetables together in a large bowl with the butter.

Lay the vegetables on a cookie sheet and roast for 6–7 minutes, until they are nicely browned. Season with salt and pepper.

Herb Butter

2 cups	butter, softened to room temperature	475 mL
½	lemon, juice only	½
1 Tbsp.	chopped chives	15 mL
1 Tbsp.	chopped parsley	15 mL
½ Tbsp.	chopped thyme	7.5 mL
	salt and freshly ground black pepper to taste	

With a spatula, whip the butter. Add the lemon juice, herbs, salt and pepper. Mix well.

Lay a piece of plastic wrap on your work surface. Place half of the butter on the wrap and roll into a log. Twist the ends of the wrap closed. Repeat with the rest of the butter.

Freeze for up to 2 months.

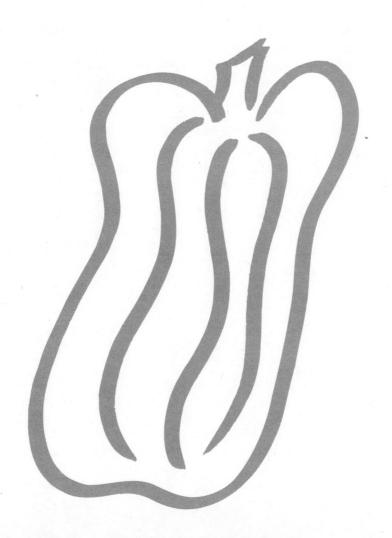

Grilled Seasonal Vegetables

Serves 8

1	bulb fennel, cut in half	1
1½ cups	zucchini, cut diagonally into ⅜-inch (1-cm) slices	360 mL
2½ cups	red, orange and yellow bell peppers, cut in half	600 mL
1½ cups	Japanese eggplant, cut diagonally into ⅜-inch (1-cm) slices	360 mL
1½ cups	portobello mushrooms cut into 6 wedges and gills removed	360 mL
¼ cup	olive oil	60 mL
	salt and freshly ground black pepper to taste	

We normally serve these vegetables at room temperature dressed with a little balsamic vinaigrette.

Preheat the barbecue or broiler to hot.

Toss the vegetables in olive oil. Grill over high heat till tender but not mushy. The zucchini will only take about 3 minutes, followed by the peppers, eggplant and portobello mushrooms. The fennel will take the longest to grill, about 7–8 minutes.

Remove the vegetables to a serving platter. When they have cooled, season with salt and pepper and toss lightly with a balsamic vinaigrette, using 1 part vinegar to 4 parts olive oil.

Wild Mushroom Terrine

Serves 8

8	potatoes	8
4 cups	mixed wild mushrooms (portobello,	950 mL
	shiitake, button and oyster)	
	salt and freshly ground black	
	pepper to taste	
1½–2 cups	Vegetable Stock (page 168)	360–475 mL

Preheat the oven to 350°F (175°C). Grease a 9- x 13-inch (22- x 33-cm) glass baking dish.

Peel and thinly slice the potatoes (a mandoline is the best tool for this). Thinly slice the mushrooms.

Cover the bottom of the baking dish with ½ inch (1.2 cm) of potatoes. Place all the mushrooms on top and cover with another ½ inch (1.2 cm) of potatoes. Season with salt and pepper. Pour the vegetable stock over all to a depth of ½ inch (1.2 cm).

Oil one side of a sheet of aluminum foil and lightly cover the potatoes, oiled side down. Bake for 1 hour, then remove the foil. Bake another 30–45 minutes, or until a knife goes through the center easily. Remove from the oven. Place a heavy object on top of the terrine to compress it while cooling, for about 1 hour.

To serve, cut the terrine into squares, place on a greased cookie sheet and reheat at 350°F (175°C) for 10–15 minutes.

Here's a great no-fat side dish, full of flavor and textures.

Basic Mashed Potatoes

Serves 8

5	medium yellow-fleshed potatoes (Yukon Gold are excellent)	5
4 Tbsp.	butter, unsalted	60 mL
4 Tbsp.	whipping cream	60 mL
	salt and white pepper to taste	

Peel the potatoes, cut each into 5–6 large pieces and cook in boiling salted water for about 15 minutes, or until a fork pierces them easily. Drain immediately and pass through a ricer.

Blend the butter and whipping cream into the potatoes with a wooden spoon and season to taste with salt and pepper.

Note: If you don't have a ricer, use a potato masher or a wooden fork to mash the potatoes. If using a mixer with the paddle attachment, beat for no more than 10–12 revolutions of the paddle at low speed.

Simple mashed potatoes with cream and butter are a homey delight. For a twist, dress them up with fresh herbs.

Saffron Mash: Add a pinch of saffron to the whipping cream and bring to a boil. Cool slightly and blend into the potatoes with the butter. Wonderful served with sea bass.

Leek and Dijon Mustard Mash: Sauté 1 cup (240 mL) chopped leeks, white parts only, in olive oil. Add to the mashed potatoes with 2 tsp. (10 mL) Dijon mustard.

Roasted Garlic Mash: Mince 2 Tbsp. (30 mL) of roasted garlic and add to the mashed potatoes.

White Cheddar and Roasted Corn Mash: Roast 1 cup (240 mL) corn kernels in a 400°F (200°C) oven for 10 minutes. Add to the mashed potatoes with ½ cup (120 mL) of grated white Cheddar cheese.

Curried Sweet Potato Mash: Use sweet potatoes instead of regular potatoes. Cook 1 Tbsp. (15 mL) curry powder in oil and blend into the potatoes with the butter and whipping cream.

Beet Mash: Substitute 2 cooked beets for 2 of the potatoes in the basic recipe.

Garlic Rosemary New Potatoes

Serves 8

12 cups	baby red potatoes cut into thirds or quarters, depending on size	3 L
⅓ cup	olive oil	80 mL
4 Tbsp.	minced garlic	60 mL
2 Tbsp.	rosemary leaves	30 mL
	salt and freshly ground black pepper to taste	

Preheat the oven to 375°F (190°C).

Blanch the potatoes in boiling salted water for about 5 minutes, or approximately 1 minute after the water returns to a boil. Drain and pat dry with paper towels.

Toss the potatoes with the olive oil, garlic, rosemary, salt and pepper.

Place on a baking sheet and roast until golden brown, approximately 25 minutes. Toss occasionally to brown on all sides.

These potatoes are also delicious with whole cloves of garlic roasted with them.

Caramelized Winter Vegetables

Serves 8

1½ cups	beets, cut into ¾-inch (2-cm) cubes	360 mL
1 cup	rutabaga or yellow turnips, cut into ¾-inch (2-cm) cubes	240 mL
1 cup	yams, cut into ¾-inch (2-cm) cubes	240 mL
1 cup	sweet potatoes, cut into ¾-inch (2-cm) cubes	240 mL
1½ cups	carrots, cut diagonally into ¼-inch (.6-cm) pieces	360 mL
2 cups	green beans, trimmed	475 mL
6 Tbsp.	vegetable oil	90 mL
	salt and freshly ground black pepper to taste	

High-heat roasting is the key to success in this recipe. The vegetables are pre-blanched so that they retain their shape and color, even after the quick roasting.

Preheat the oven to 450°F (230°C).

Blanch all the vegetables separately in boiling salted water, for about 5 minutes each. Drain. Refresh in ice water and drain.

Toss each vegetable in about 1 Tbsp. (15 mL) of oil and season with salt and black pepper.

Place the vegetables separately on cookie sheets and roast for about 7–8 minutes, until the vegetables are nicely browned.

To serve, arrange the vegetables attractively on a platter.

Root Vegetable Gratin

Serves 8

5	medium potatoes, peeled	5
1–2	medium yams, peeled	1–2
1–2	medium sweet potatoes, peeled	1–2
2	small rutabagas, peeled	2
2 cups	whipping cream	475 mL
2 cups	half-and-half cream	475 mL
2 Tbsp.	minced garlic	30 mL
1 tsp.	salt	5 mL
1 tsp.	white pepper	5 mL

Thinly slice the vegetables (a mandoline is the best tool for this). Set aside.

In a saucepan, scald the creams (until hot to the touch) with the garlic, salt and pepper.

Preheat the oven to 350°F (175°C).

In a greased 9- x 13-inch (23- x 33-cm) glass baking dish, assemble the layers in this order: potatoes, yams, potatoes, sweet potatoes, potatoes and rutabaga.

Pour the scalded cream over all. Bake for 1¼–1½ hours, until a knife goes through easily.

Let rest for 10 minutes. Cut into squares and serve hot.

A simple-to-make vegetable accompaniment for a festive meal, this is colorful, full of vitamins and packed with flavor.

Green Beans with Hazelnut Brown Butter

Serves 8

1½ lbs.	green beans, trimmed	680 g
⅓ cup	hazelnuts, toasted and chopped (see Toasting Nuts, page 173)	80 mL
⅓ cup	butter	80 mL
	salt and freshly ground black pepper to taste	

A simple yet elegant side dish to serve with any dinner entrée. Preparing this side dish will give you time to concentrate on the main course.

Blanch the green beans in boiling salted water for 3 minutes. Drain and cover with ice water to stop further cooking. Drain the beans and place them on a baking sheet.

Preheat the broiler.

Melt the butter in a saucepan and heat until it is lightly brown and gives off a nutty aroma. Add the hazelnuts, remove from the heat and stir.

Place the baking sheet under the broiler for about 3 minutes, or until the beans are hot and crispy. Reheat the hazelnut butter over low heat for about 1 minute and spoon over the hot beans.

Wild Rice Pilaf

Serves 8

2 cups	white or brown rice	475 mL
2 cups	wild rice	475 mL
4 Tbsp.	butter	60 mL
½ cup	red peppers, cut into ¼-inch (.6-cm) dice	120 mL
½ cup	sliced button mushrooms	120 mL
½ cup	chopped green onions zest of 1 orange	120 mL
2 Tbsp.	soy sauce	30 mL

Cook the 2 kinds of rice separately according to package directions and set aside. Keep warm over low heat.

In a medium pot melt the butter. Add the red peppers, mushrooms, green onions and orange zest. Sauté for 5 minutes.

Add the rice and heat for 2 minutes while stirring. Stir in the soy sauce. Taste and adjust the seasoning with salt and pepper if necessary.

This is a great standard rice dish that is easy to prepare and always a favorite.

desserts

White Chocolate Mousse Bombe

Serves 8 to 10

Base

4 oz.	semi-sweet chocolate	113 g
½ cup	butter	120 mL
1 cup	sugar	240 mL
2	egg yolks	2
3 Tbsp.	hot water	45 mL
½ cup	all-purpose flour	120 mL
2	egg whites	2

This dessert looks complicated but is very easy to make. You'll wow your guests with this recipe!

Chocolate Plastique Topping

6 oz.	semi-sweet chocolate	170 g
4 Tbsp.	corn syrup	60 mL

Filling

1⅔ cups	whipping cream	400 mL
9 oz.	chopped white chocolate	255 g

Preheat the oven to 350°F (175°C). Line the bottom of a 9-inch (23-cm) springform pan with parchment paper.

Melt the 4 oz. (113 g) semi-sweet chocolate in a double boiler or microwave and let cool.

Cream the butter with the sugar. Slowly blend in the egg yolks. Add the melted chocolate to the sugar mixture, then add the hot water and mix well. Add the flour and mix until just blended.

Beat the egg whites until soft peaks form. Fold into the chocolate mixture. Pour into the springform pan.

Bake for 20 minutes. Do not overbake. Cool on a rack.

For the topping, melt the 6 oz. (170 g) semi-sweet chocolate in a double boiler. Add the corn syrup and mix until blended. Form the mixture into a ball. Place it between two sheets of waxed paper and roll with a rolling pin until it is 16 inches (38 cm) in diameter. Leaving it between the waxed paper, place it in the refrigerator. It will remain pliable when cooled.

Heat the whipping cream until it's steaming. Pour the cream over the white chocolate and whisk thoroughly. Chill for 3 hours or, for better results, overnight in the fridge. When it's fully chilled, whip it with an electric mixer until thickened.

Scoop the white chocolate mousse over the chocolate base and mold it into a dome shape. Place it back in the fridge until well set, about 1 hour.

Carefully remove the cake from the pan and set it on a serving platter. Remove the rolled chocolate from the fridge and center it on top of the cake. Gently press the chocolate around the cake and cut off the excess at the base.

Save the pieces that you cut away from the chocolate plastique topping. You can make decorations, such as stars or roses, to decorate the top of the bombe.

Sweet Dough

Makes 2 9-inch (23-cm) tart shells

2 cups	all-purpose flour	475 mL
⅓ cup	sugar	80 mL
1 cup	soft butter	240 mL
2	egg yolks	2

Preheat the oven to 350°F (175°C).

Combine the flour and sugar. With a pastry cutter, blend in the butter until it forms coarse crumbs.

Add the yolks one at a time, mixing only until the dough comes away from the sides of the bowl.

Roll into 2 balls. Flatten and wrap in plastic wrap. Chill until needed.

I prefer to use this sweet dough for flans. It is really no-fail; however, if you underbake it, it doesn't taste quite as good. You want a light glow like short-bread for it to taste its best.

Lemon Citron Tarte

Serves 8

½ recipe	Sweet Dough (page 128)	½ recipe
6 Tbsp.	blanched almonds	90 mL
3 Tbsp.	sugar	45 mL
3	eggs	3
1 cup	sugar	240 mL
¾ cup	freshly squeezed lemon juice	180 mL
1 tsp.	finely grated lemon zest	5 mL
½ cup	melted butter, less 1 Tbsp. (15 mL)	105 mL

Preheat the oven to 325°F (165°C).

Grease a 9-inch (23-cm) tart pan and line the bottom with a piece of parchment. On a floured surface, roll the sweet dough into a circle ⅛ inch (.3 cm) thick. Fit the pastry into the pan, trimming the excess away with a sharp knife. Line the shell with a piece of foil and weigh it down with some grain or beans. Bake the shell until slightly golden, 12–15 minutes. Remove the foil and grain or beans.

Pulverize the almonds with the 3 Tbsp. (45 mL) sugar in a blender or food processor until a fine powder is obtained.

Using a whisk, whisk the eggs and 1 cup (240 mL) sugar until well blended.

Stir in the lemon juice and zest. Add the almond powder and melted butter, mixing well.

Pour into the flan shell and bake for 30 minutes, until firm to the touch. Watch that it doesn't brown.

Thanks to Deborah Roitberg and her family for this sensational recipe. Customers have been begging me for the secret, and here it is at last!

Macadamia and Coconut Tarte

Serves 8

½ recipe	Sweet Dough (page 128)	½ recipe
½ cup	flaked unsweetened coconut	120 mL
1 cup	macadamia nuts	240 mL
6 Tbsp.	butter	90 mL
3 Tbsp.	honey	45 mL
3 Tbsp.	whipping cream	45 mL
¾ cup	brown sugar	180 mL
3	egg yolks	3
1 tsp.	vanilla extract	5 mL

This is like a giant Hawaiian butter tart.

Preheat the oven to 325°F (165°C).

Grease a 9-inch (23-cm) tart pan and line the bottom with a circle of parchment. On a floured surface, roll the sweet dough into a circle ⅛ inch (.3 cm) thick. Fit the pastry into the pan, trimming the excess away with a sharp knife. Line the shell with a piece of foil and weigh it down with some grain or beans. Bake the shell until slightly golden, 12–15 minutes. Remove the foil and grain or beans.

Increase the oven temperature to 350°F (175°C).

On a baking sheet, toast the coconut until golden brown, about 5–7 minutes. Stir occasionally for even toasting. Set aside.

On a separate baking sheet, toast the macadamia nuts until golden brown, about 6–8 minutes. Cool. Chop very coarsely into ¼-inch (.6-cm) chunks and set aside. Increase the oven temperature to 375°F (190°C).

Melt the butter and honey in a saucepan. Remove from the heat.

Add the cream, sugar, egg yolks and vanilla. Whisk until blended.

Stir in the coconut and macadamia nuts, and pour into the prebaked tart shell. Bake for 20 minutes, until golden brown and just set.

Bistro Berry Crisp

Serves 10 to 12

8 cups	mixed fresh or frozen berries (blueberries, raspberries and blackberries)	2 L
1¼ cups	granulated sugar	300 mL
¼ cup	cornstarch (use 2 Tbsp./30 mL if berries are fresh)	60 mL
1 tsp.	lemon juice	5 mL
¼ tsp.	nutmeg	1.2 mL
¾ cup	cold butter	180 mL
1 cup	flour	240 mL
1 cup	brown sugar	240 mL
½ cup	oats	120 mL
1½ tsp.	cinnamon	7.5 mL

Preheat the oven to 375°F (190°C).

Mix the berries, granulated sugar, cornstarch, lemon juice and nutmeg. Pour into a 9- x 13-inch (23- x 33-cm) casserole dish.

Cube the butter and blend with the flour and brown sugar until crumbly. Add the oats and cinnamon. Spread the mixture over the berries.

Bake for 40–45 minutes, or until the fruit is bubbly and the top is crisp.

This is such a simple recipe and the fruits do all the work by providing extra-ordinary flavors.

Chocolate Caramel Mousse Cake

Serves 10 to 12

Shortbread Base

½ cup	cold butter	120 mL
½ cup	all-purpose flour	120 mL
¼ cup	sugar	60 mL
¼ cup	all-purpose flour	60 mL
1	egg yolk	1

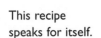

This recipe speaks for itself.

Caramel Nut Layer

2 cups	hazelnuts, toasted (see Toasting Nuts, page 173)	475 mL
1½ cups	sugar	360 mL
1 cup	water	240 mL
5–6 Tbsp.	whipping cream	75–90 mL

Mousse Layer

6 cups	whipping cream	1.5 L
24 oz.	semi-sweet chocolate, coarsely chopped	680 g

Preheat the oven to 350°F (175°C).

In a food processor or with a pastry cutter, process the butter, ½ cup (120 mL) flour and sugar until pea-sized lumps are formed. Mix the ¼ cup (60 mL) flour with the egg yolk and add to the mixture. Process until blended or crumbly.

Press the mixture into a 10-inch (25-cm) springform pan. Bake for 25 minutes, until slightly golden. Cool on a rack.

Coarsely chop the hazelnuts in a food processor (the nuts should be chunky). Combine the sugar and water in a saucepan. Cook over medium-high heat without stirring until it begins to brown, then swirl the pot, but do not stir the mixture. Continue heating without stirring, to a rich brown color.

Remove from the heat and gradually whisk in the cream. Add the toasted hazelnuts. Pour the caramel over the cooled shortbread crust and let set until the caramel is room temperature.

To make the mousse, heat the whipping cream until it's simmering. Pour it over the chopped chocolate and stir until all the chocolate is melted. Strain. Chill for 2–3 hours in the fridge until set, or overnight.

When it's fully chilled, beat the mousse with an electric mixer until thickened. Spoon over the caramel nut layer and smooth.

Chill for 2 hours. When set, slide a thin knife around the inside of the springform pan and release the sides.

Dust with cocoa powder or sprinkle with milk chocolate shavings.

The Famous Lazy Gourmet Cheesecake

Serves 8 to 10

Base

⅓ cup	butter	80 mL
¼ cup	brown sugar	60 mL
1 ⅓ cups	graham wafer crumbs	320 mL

Filling

1 lb.	cream cheese, room temperature	455 g
⅔ cup	granulated sugar	160 mL
½ cup	sour cream	120 mL
¼ cup	whipping cream	60 mL
3	eggs	3
1 Tbsp.	orange liqueur, preferably Cointreau	15 mL

Topping

1 cup	sour cream	240 mL
4 Tbsp.	granulated sugar	60 mL
2 tsp.	orange liqueur, preferably Cointreau	10 mL

This cheesecake and its chocolate variation launched my career. My friend, the late Larry Lillo, used to trick me into making cheesecake for him by offering to give constructive criticism in order to perfect the recipe. For a chocolate cheesecake, melt 7 oz. (200 g) semi-sweet chocolate in a double boiler. Cool slightly and mix well with the cream cheese filling. Try Frangelico, Amaretto or mint liqueur for a different flavor. Decorate with chocolate shavings.

Preheat the oven to 350°F (175°C).

Lightly butter a 9-inch (23-cm) springform pan. Melt the butter in a saucepan. Mix in the brown sugar. Add the graham wafer crumbs and mix thoroughly. Press into the bottom of the pan. Bake for 5 minutes. Cool on a rack.

Reduce the oven temperature to 250°F (120°C).

For the filling, beat the cream cheese and ⅔ cup (160 mL) granulated sugar until smooth. Add the sour cream and cream. Add the eggs one at a time, beating each addition well. Stir in the orange liqueur. Pour the mixture over the crust and bake for 30–40 minutes, or until set.

For the topping, combine the sour cream, 4 Tbsp. (60 mL) granulated sugar and orange liqueur. Pour over the cheesecake. Spread gently to cover the top completely. Return to the oven for 5 minutes. Remove and chill for at least 2–3 hours before serving.

Skor Bar Cake

Serves 16

3 cups	flour	720 mL
2 tsp.	baking powder	10 mL
7	Skor chocolate bars, chopped	7
1 cup	butter, softened	240 mL
3 Tbsp.	vegetable shortening	45 mL
1⅞ cups	berry sugar	450 mL
4	eggs	4
1 Tbsp.	vanilla	15 mL
1 cup	milk	240 mL

Preheat the oven to 350°F (175°C).

In a bowl, combine the flour and baking powder. Toss 2 Tbsp. (30 mL) of the flour mixture with the Skor pieces.

In a large bowl, cream the butter and shortening well. Add the sugar slowly, then add the eggs one at a time, beating well after each addition. Add the vanilla and beat for 5 minutes.

Beat in one-third of the flour mixture, then half the milk, beating well after each addition. Repeat with one-third of the flour and the remaining milk, finishing with the remaining flour. Fold in the Skor pieces and pour into a bundt pan.

Bake for 55 minutes. Cool. Invert, remove from the pan and cool completely.

This is a cake made only on special occasions, like my birthday and my daughter's. Thanks to Deborah Roitberg for the recipe. Another winner!

Sour Cream Blueberry Bundt

Serves 8 to 10

Bundt

1 cup	butter	240 mL
2 cups	granulated sugar	475 mL
2	eggs	2
1 cup	sour cream	240 mL
1 tsp.	vanilla	5 mL
2 cups	sifted cake flour	475 mL
1 tsp.	baking powder	5 mL
½ tsp	salt	2.5 mL
1 cup	blueberries	240 mL
2 Tbsp.	all-purpose flour	30 mL

This has got to be one of the moistest coffee cakes in existence.

Topping

1 cup	chopped pecans	240 mL
2 Tbsp.	granulated sugar	30 mL
1 tsp.	cinnamon	5 mL
½ tsp.	nutmeg (optional)	2.5 mL

Glaze

1½ cups	confectioners' sugar	360 mL
2 Tbsp.	butter	30 mL
1 tsp.	vanilla	5 mL
1–2 Tbsp.	hot water	15–30 mL

Preheat the oven to 325°F (165°C). Grease a bundt pan.

Cream the butter and add the sugar gradually, beating until light. Add the eggs one at a time, beating until fluffy. Mix in the sour cream and vanilla.

Sift together the 2 cups (475 mL) cake flour, baking powder and salt. Add to the creamed mixture. Lightly toss the blueberries in the 2 Tbsp. (30 mL) flour and fold into the batter.

In another bowl, combine the topping ingredients.

Pour half the batter into the prepared bundt pan. Sprinkle with half the topping mixture. Add the remaining batter and finish with the remaining topping.

Bake for 1 hour, or until a cake tester comes out clean from the center of the cake.

Cool in the pan for 10 minutes. Turn out onto a rack and let cool. Combine the glaze ingredients, stirring until smooth. Drizzle over the cake.

Banana Bread Pudding

Serves 10 to 12

3 cups	whipping cream	720 mL
4 cups	cubed sweet bread, such as banana loaf, challah, or croissant (do not use breads with grains or seeds)	950 mL
10	eggs	10
1¾ cups	packed brown sugar	420 mL
1 Tbsp.	vanilla	15 mL
1 tsp.	cinnamon	5 mL
1 tsp.	nutmeg	5 mL
3 cups	mashed fresh bananas	720 mL

A favorite of my mother, Roz! Banana lovers can't get enough of this dessert. Try throwing in a cup of white chocolate chunks to add flavor and calories!

Preheat the oven to 350°F (175°C).

Pour the whipping cream over the bread in a large bowl. Set aside and allow to soak through.

In a separate bowl, combine the eggs, sugar, vanilla, cinnamon, nutmeg and bananas. Add the mixture to the soaked bread. Fold in until well blended. Pour into a greased 9- x 13-inch (23- x 33-cm) glass baking dish. Cover with aluminum foil.

Set the baking dish into a roasting pan. Fill the pan with enough water to come halfway up the sides of the baking dish. Bake for approximately 40 minutes until a knife inserted into the center comes out clean. Remove the foil for the last 5 minutes of the cooking time to allow the top to brown. Serve warm.

Triple Chocolate Bread Pudding

Serves 10 to 12

3 cups	whipping cream	720 mL
4 cups	cubed sweet bread, such as challah, croissants, scones or leftover chocolate cake	950 mL
10	eggs	10
1¾ cups	sugar	420 mL
1 Tbsp.	vanilla	15 mL
2 Tbsp.	cocoa powder	30 mL
1 tsp.	nutmeg	5 mL
5½ oz.	semi-sweet chocolate chips	155 g
5½ oz.	white chocolate chips	155 g
5½ oz.	milk chocolate chips	155 g
1 recipe	Chocolate Sauce	1 recipe

Preheat the oven to 350°F (175°C).

Pour the whipping cream over the bread in a large bowl. Set aside and allow to soak through.

In a separate bowl, combine the eggs, sugar, vanilla, cocoa and nutmeg. Mix into the soaked bread until it's well blended. Add the chocolate chips and mix well. Pour into a greased 9- x 13-inch (23- x 33-cm) glass baking dish. Cover with aluminum foil.

Set the baking dish into a roasting pan. Fill the roasting pan with enough water to come halfway up the sides of the baking dish. Bake for approximately 40 minutes until a knife inserted in the center comes out clean. Remove the foil for the last 5 minutes of the cooking time to allow the top to brown. Serve warm with chocolate sauce.

Bread puddings are a great way to use up leftover bread. Just store it in the freezer until you're ready to use it.

Chocolate Sauce

1 cup	whipping cream	240 mL
9 oz.	dark chocolate chips	255 g

Bring the cream to a boil. Add the chocolate and stir until it's melted and the sauce is smooth.

Summer Berry Bread Pudding

Serves 10 to 12

3 cups	whipping cream	720 mL
4 cups	cubed sweet bread, such as challah, croissant or scones	950 mL
10	eggs	10
1¾ cups	granulated or berry sugar	420 mL
1 Tbsp.	vanilla	15 mL
1 tsp.	nutmeg	5 mL
1 tsp.	cinnamon	5 mL
1 cup	fresh or frozen blueberries	240 mL
1 cup	fresh or frozen raspberries	240 mL
1 cup	fresh or frozen strawberries	240 mL
¼ cup	orange liqueur, preferably Cointreau	60 mL

This recipe is courtesy of our pastry chef, Dana Blundell. She makes many different varia-tions of bread pudding for the bistro. This one is very light in flavor and filled with loads of juicy berries.

Preheat the oven to 350°F (175°C). Pour the whipping cream over the bread in a large bowl. Set aside and allow to soak through.

In a separate bowl, mix together the eggs, sugar, vanilla, nutmeg and cinnamon. Mix into the soaked bread and blend well. Fold in the berries and orange liqueur. Pour into a greased 9- x 13-inch (23- x 33-cm) glass baking dish. Cover with aluminum foil.

Set the baking dish into a roasting pan. Fill the pan with enough water to come halfway up the sides of the baking dish. Bake for approximately 40 minutes, or until a knife inserted in the center comes out clean. Remove the foil for the last 5 minutes of cooking time to allow the top to brown. Serve warm with Raspberry Coulis.

Raspberry Coulis

2 cups	fresh or frozen raspberries	475 mL
¼ cup	granulated or berry sugar	60 mL
1 Tbsp.	lemon juice	15 mL
	pinch of nutmeg	
2 Tbsp.	cornstarch	30 mL
½ Tbsp.	water	7.5 mL

In a saucepan, bring the raspberries, sugar, lemon juice and nut-meg to a boil. Reduce the heat to low.

Mix the cornstarch and water together. Add to the raspberry mixture. Cook, stirring constantly, until the mixture thickens, about 2 minutes.

Lazy Gourmet's Lava Cakes

Serves 8

¾ cup	butter	180 mL
½ lb.	semi-sweet chocolate	225 g
½ cup	sugar	120 mL
3 Tbsp.	cornstarch	45 mL
4	eggs	4
4	egg yolks	4

Melt the butter and chocolate in a saucepan over low heat. Mix the sugar and cornstarch together in a bowl. Crack the eggs into another bowl and whisk the yolks into the whole eggs.

When the chocolate has melted, remove from the heat. Whisk in the sugar-cornstarch mixture until blended. Add the eggs and stir until smooth. Chill in the fridge overnight.

Preheat the oven to 400°F (200°C). Line a baking sheet with parchment paper.

Line 8 metal rings (you can use a 1½-inch-deep (3.8-cm) tin can with both ends opened) with a strip of parchment paper, or grease ½-cup (120-mL) ramekins. Set the rings on the baking sheet and brush generously with butter. Scoop the chocolate filling into each one, filling them ⅔ full.

Bake in the oven for 12–15 minutes.

Remove from the oven. Slide a metal spatula under the cakes and transfer to serving plates. Gently slide the rings off the cakes and remove the parchment. Dust with icing sugar and serve immediately.

Thanks to our Hawaiian friend Michael Rabe for sending this recipe from Hawaii. The only glitch that can happen with these is that the lava cakes ooze before they get to your guests. At home I make them in ramekins to avoid this problem, but the presentation is not quite as good.

Crème Brulée

Serves 4

2 cups	whipping cream	475 mL
⅓ cup	granulated sugar	80 mL
½	vanilla bean (split lengthwise)	½
4	egg yolks	4
1 Tbsp.	brown sugar	15 mL
9 Tbsp.	granulated sugar	135 mL

Preheat the oven to 350°F (175°C).

Combine the cream, ⅓ cup (80 mL) granulated sugar and vanilla bean in a saucepan and bring to a boil. Cool slightly. Discard the vanilla bean.

Beat the egg yolks together. Slowly add the hot cream to the yolks, beating vigorously with a whisk. Pour the mixture through a fine sieve.

Pour into individual glass or porcelain ramekins (approximately 5 oz./140 g). Place the ramekins in a shallow baking pan. Fill the pan with water until it reaches halfway up the sides of the ramekins. Cover the pan with aluminum foil.

Bake for 1 hour, or until the custards are set but still jiggle in the middle. Cool on a rack, then remove from the pan and refrigerate for at least 1 hour, until chilled.

To serve, combine the brown sugar and 9 Tbsp. (135 mL) granulated sugar and sprinkle evenly over the surface of the custards. Brown evenly with a blowtorch or under the broiler. Be sure to only brown, or caramelize, the sugar, not to burn it.

Star Anise: Add 5–6 broken star anise to the cream. Discard before combining with the egg yolks.

Espresso: Add ½ cup (120 mL) espresso beans to the cream. Discard before combining with the egg yolks.

Pumpkin: Add 1 cup (240 mL) pumpkin purée, ½ tsp. (2.5 mL) cinnamon and ¼ tsp. (1.2 mL) nutmeg to the egg yolks.

You can make the traditional version, or change the flavor with simple variations. Even those on diets will occasionally indulge in this popular dessert!

squares & cookies

The Original Nanaimo Bars

Makes 20 bars

Base

¾ cup	butter	180 mL
⅓ cup	granulated sugar	80 mL
2 Tbsp.	cocoa powder	30 mL
2	eggs	2
1 tsp.	vanilla	5 mL
3 cups	graham wafer crumbs	720 mL
1½ cups	coconut	360 mL
½ cup	chopped walnuts (optional)	120 mL

Custard Layer

6 Tbsp.	butter, softened	90 mL
¼ cup	milk	60 mL
3 cups	icing sugar	720 mL
3 Tbsp.	custard powder	45 mL
½ tsp.	vanilla	2.5 mL

Topping

10 oz.	semi-sweet chocolate	284 g
2 Tbsp.	butter	30 mL

The Lazy Gourmet was the first establishment to commercially sell Nanaimo bars in 1979! Now they are everywhere. We make our N.B.s (as we call them) without nuts so that people with nut allergies can enjoy them too.

For the base, melt the butter, and combine it with the sugar and cocoa powder in the top of a double boiler. Beat the eggs and add to the mixture. Stir until slightly thickened, about 2 minutes. Add the vanilla. Stir in the graham wafer crumbs, coconut and nuts, if desired, until well combined. Press the mixture evenly into a 9- x 13-inch (23- x 33-cm) greased baking pan. Let stand 15 minutes.

For the custard layer, cream the butter, milk, icing sugar, custard powder and vanilla. Spread evenly on top of the base layer. Refrigerate for 15 minutes.

For the topping, melt the chocolate in the top of a double boiler. Stir the butter in gently until just blended. Spread over the custard layer and chill in the fridge.

To cut the squares without cracking the chocolate, always slice the squares when they are at room temperature. Use a fine-tipped paring knife. Cut partway through first, then cut all the way through.

Million Dollar Bars

Makes 40 bars

1 cup	granulated sugar	240 mL
1 cup	brown sugar	240 mL
1½ cups	cold butter	360 mL
2	egg yolks	2
½ tsp.	vanilla	2.5 mL
2 cups	flour	475 mL
	pinch salt	
10 oz.	milk chocolate	285 mL
1 cup	flaked almonds	240 mL

Preheat the oven to 350°F (175°C). Grease a 12- x 17-inch (30- x 43-cm) jelly-roll pan.

In a mixing bowl or food processor, cream the sugars with the butter at medium speed. Add the eggs one at a time, then the vanilla. Switch the speed to low and mix in the flour and salt.

Using the heel of your hand or a rolling pin, flatten the mixture into the prepared pan. Bake for 45 minutes in the center of the oven.

Spread the almonds on a dry baking sheet and toast lightly for 3–4 minutes in the oven.

Melt the chocolate in the top of a double boiler. Spread on the warm baked dough. Sprinkle the nuts over the top.

Cut into 2-inch (5-cm) squares while still warm.

I don't know how it came to be known as the Million Dollar Bar, but with its choco-almond crunchiness, it is a terrific pick-me-up snack. Guaranteed to make you feel like a million bucks.

145

Black and White Brownies

Makes 16 brownies

Base

6 oz.	semi-sweet chocolate	170 g
¾ cup	butter	180 mL
1 cup	sugar	240 mL
3	eggs	3
¾ cup	all-purpose flour	180 mL

Cream Cheese Topping

1 lb.	cream cheese	454 g
⅔ cup	sugar	160 mL
4	eggs	4
1 tsp.	vanilla	5 mL

This is a combination cheesecake and square rolled into one. The squares are firmer and cut more easily than cheesecake.

Preheat the oven to 325°F (165°C). Lightly grease a 9- x 13-inch (23- x 33-cm) baking pan.

For the base, melt the chocolate in the top of a double boiler. Remove from the heat and let cool to lukewarm. Beat the butter and sugar together. Add the eggs, one at a time. Mix in the chocolate, but do not overbeat. Fold in the flour.

Reserve 1 cup (240 mL) of the batter and spread the remainder into the prepared pan.

For the topping, mix the cream cheese and sugar together. Add the eggs one at a time, beating well with each addition. Mix in the vanilla. Spread the cream cheese mixture over the base.

Drop the reserved batter by spoonfuls over the cream cheese mixture. Swirl to create a marbled effect.

Bake for 40–45 minutes, or until set. Cool on a rack and refrigerate until firm. Cut into squares. Keep in the fridge until serving time.

Sweet and Tart Lemon Squares

Makes 16 squares

Base

1½ cups	all-purpose flour	360 mL
6 Tbsp.	sugar	90 mL
¾ cup	butter	180 mL

Topping

5	large eggs	5
2	egg yolks	2
2½ cups	sugar	600 mL
1 cup	freshly squeezed lemon juice	240 mL
¼ cup	flour	60 mL

Preheat the oven to 350°F (175°C). Grease a 9- x 13-inch (23- x 33-cm) baking pan.

For the base, mix the flour, sugar and butter together until well combined. Press the mixture evenly into the prepared pan. Bake for 18–20 minutes, or until light golden.

To make the topping, beat the egg yolks, eggs and sugar together until smooth. Stir in the lemon juice, then add the flour.

Pour over the baked crust and bake for approximately 40 minutes, or until set. Cool on a rack, then chill in the fridge for at least 2 hours, so that the custard is firmly set. Use a thin paring knife to cut it into small squares.

Freshly squeezed lemon juice is what makes this square so special. Don't be put off by the amount of sugar. Keep in mind how much lemon juice is in the recipe!

cover loosely with foil until last 7 mins.

Rocky Roads

Makes 20 squares

1 cup	butter	240 mL
2 lbs.	semi-sweet chocolate, melted	900 g
1	10-oz. (285-g) bag mini marshmallows	1
1½ cups	hazelnuts, toasted (see Toasting Nuts, page 173)	360 mL
2 cups	whole almonds, toasted (see Toasting Nuts, page 173)	475 mL

Preheat the oven to 350°F (175°C). Lightly grease a 9- x 13-inch (23- x 33-cm) baking pan.

Melt the butter and chocolate in the top of a double boiler. Allow to cool.

Stir the marshmallows and nuts into the cooled chocolate mixture. Spread into the prepared pan. Refrigerate for 2–3 hours. Cut into small squares.

I first tried this decadence at a bagel deli. Two years later I bought the deli on the condition of getting this recipe. Now you know that these squares are worth over six figures. Enjoy!

Peanut Butter Candy Cookies

Makes 12 to 18 cookies

1 cup	peanut butter	240 mL
1 cup	butter, softened	240 mL
1⅓ cups	granulated sugar	320 mL
1⅓ cups	brown sugar	320 mL
2	eggs	2
1 tsp.	vanilla	5 mL
3 cups	flour	720 mL
1 tsp.	baking powder	5 mL
1 tsp.	baking soda	5 mL
1 cup	Smarties or M&M's	240 mL

Preheat the oven to 350°F (175°C). Line a baking sheet with parchment paper.

Blend the peanut butter and butter until smooth. Add the granulated and brown sugars and cream well. Add the eggs and vanilla, blending well.

Sift the flour, baking powder and baking soda together, and stir into the peanut butter mixture.

Shape into 2-inch (5-cm) balls. Place on the prepared baking sheet and flatten with a fork. Press 3–4 Smarties or M&M's onto the top of each cookie.

Bake for 10–12 minutes, until golden but not brown. Cool on a rack.

Make giant or small cookies. At home, I find that only the smaller ones fit into the cookie jar.

Ginger Cookies

Makes 6 dozen

1 cup	butter, softened	240 mL
1 cup	brown sugar	240 mL
¼ cup	molasses	60 mL
2	egg whites	2
2⅔ cups	flour	640 mL
1 tsp.	cinnamon	5 mL
1 tsp.	ginger	5 mL
½ tsp.	cloves	2.5 mL
½ tsp.	salt	2.5 mL
2 tsp.	baking soda	10 mL

Preheat the oven to 375°F (190°C). Grease a baking sheet.

Cream the butter in a large bowl. Add the sugar and beat until well blended. Add the molasses and egg whites. Set aside.

Sift the cinnamon, ginger, cloves, salt and baking soda with the flour. Add to the butter mixture, blending well.

Wrap the dough in plastic wrap and refrigerate for 1 hour.

Shape into small balls (2-inch/5-cm), place on the prepared baking sheet and flatten. Sprinkle with granulated sugar. Bake for 10 minutes, until firm. Cool on a rack.

We spent a long time in pursuit of the world's greatest ginger cookie. It took us down many paths—and we stopped here! Thanks to Nicole Mindell, who didn't stop until the job was done.

Chocolate Macaroons

Makes 12 to 14 macaroons

4 oz.	melted semi-sweet chocolate	113 g
¾ cup	white sugar	180 mL
2½ cups	shredded sweetened coconut (not desiccated)	600 mL
¼ cup	cocoa powder	60 mL
3	large egg whites	3
1 tsp.	vanilla	5 mL
	pinch salt	

Preheat the oven to 325°F (165°C). Line a cookie sheet with parchment paper.

Melt the chocolate in the top of a double boiler. Set aside.

Combine the sugar, coconut, cocoa, egg whites, vanilla and salt until well blended. Add the melted chocolate and stir until the coconut is well coated. Drop by small spoonfuls onto the prepared cookie sheet and shape into pyramids.

Bake for about 15 minutes. Allow to cool before removing from the parchment. Store in a well-sealed dry container.

A year-round best-seller, these treats are often requested for our Christmas baking trays, though they were specifically designed for Passover.

Vanilla Macaroons

Makes 12 to 14 macaroons

¾ cup	granulated sugar	180 mL
2	large egg whites	2
2½ cups	shredded sweetened coconut	600 mL
1 tsp.	vanilla	5 mL
	pinch of salt	

Preheat the oven to 325°F (165°C). Line a cookie sheet with parchment paper.

Combine all the ingredients until well mixed. Drop by small spoonfuls onto the prepared cookie sheet and shape into pyramids.

Bake for 12–15 minutes, until lightly browned. Allow to cool before removing from the parchment. Store in a tightly sealed dry container.

A welcome treat for those with wheat allergies. Great on trays with chocolate-dipped strawberries. Pyramid shapes are perfect when using this recipe for Passover.

White Chocolate Macadamia Biscotti

Makes 12 to 16

½ cup	butter, softened	120 mL
¾ cup	sugar	180 mL
2	eggs	2
1 tsp.	vanilla	5 mL
2 Tbsp.	Amaretto liqueur	30 mL
2 cups + 2 Tbsp.	flour	505 mL
1½ tsp.	baking powder	7.5 mL
¼ tsp.	salt	1.2 mL
2 Tbsp.	shredded sweetened coconut	30 mL
⅔ cup	macadamia nuts	160 mL
⅔ cup	white chocolate chips	160 mL

Preheat the oven to 350°F (175°C). Grease a baking sheet.

Cream the butter and sugar together in a large bowl. Beat in the eggs, vanilla and Amaretto.

Sift together the flour, baking powder and salt. Add to the butter mixture. Fold in the coconut, macadamia nuts and chocolate chips.

Divide the dough into 2 pieces. On a clean surface, form each piece into a log approximately 1½ inches (4 cm) in diameter. Flatten the dough slightly and angle the ends (shaping it into a parallelogram).

Place the logs on the prepared baking sheet. Bake until just golden brown, about 30 minutes. The center will be soft. Remove from the oven and let cool for 5 minutes. Cut the biscotti diagonally into ½-inch (1.2-cm) slices. Place cut side up on the baking sheet. Bake for another 5 minutes, until golden brown. Remove and cool.

This dough is quite sticky, so use lots of flour on your work surface when forming the logs.

Almond Anise Biscotti

Makes 12 to 16

3	eggs	3
3	egg yolks	3
1 tsp.	vanilla	5 mL
1⅔ cups	sugar	400 mL
1⅓ cups	whole almonds	320 mL
2¾ cups	all-purpose flour	660 mL
½ tsp.	salt	2.5 mL
1 tsp.	baking powder	5 mL
1 tsp.	anise seeds	5 mL
	zest of 1 lemon, grated	
	zest of 1 lime, grated	
	zest of 1 orange, grated	

Can you believe that you can get a great cookie with no oil, butter or margarine? Try this!

Preheat the oven to 350°F (175°C). Grease a baking sheet.

In a large bowl, combine the eggs, egg yolks, vanilla and sugar. Add the remainder of the ingredients and mix well (the dough will be a little dry). Divide the dough into 2 pieces.

On a clean surface, form each piece of dough into a log approximately 1½ inches (4 cm) around. Press the dough flat and angle the ends (shaping it into a parallelogram). Place on the prepared baking sheet. Bake until just golden brown, about 30 minutes. The center will be soft. Remove from the oven and let cool for 5 minutes.

Cut the biscotti diagonally into ½-inch (1.2-cm) pieces. Place cut side up on the baking sheet and bake for another 5 minutes, until golden brown.

Chocolate Hazelnut Biscotti

Makes 12 to 16

2 cups	sugar	475 mL
5	eggs	5
1¾ cups	hazelnuts	420 mL
2⅔ cups	all-purpose flour	640 mL
1 cup	cocoa powder	240 mL
1½ tsp.	baking soda	7.5 mL
¼ tsp.	salt	1.2 mL
1½ Tbsp.	ground coffee	22.5 mL
⅔ cup	chocolate chips	160 mL
1½ tsp.	vanilla	7.5 mL
12 oz.	white chocolate (optional)	340 g

Preheat the oven to 350°F (175°C). Grease a baking sheet.

In a large bowl, combine the sugar and eggs. Add the rest of the ingredients, except for the white chocolate, and mix well. The dough will be dry. Divide it into 2 pieces.

On a clean surface, form each piece into a log approximately 1½ inches (4 cm) around. Press the dough flat and angle the ends (shaping it into a parallelogram). Place on the prepared baking sheet. Bake until just golden brown, about 30 minutes. The center will be soft. Remove from the oven and let cool for 5 minutes.

Cut the biscotti diagonally into ½-inch (1.2-cm) pieces. Place cut side up on the baking sheet and bake for another 5 minutes, until golden brown.

If desired, melt white chocolate in the top of a double boiler, and dip half of each biscotti into the melted chocolate.

These are great on their own or as a dunker with a cup of coffee or tea.

My Favorite Triple Chip Cookies

Makes 12 to 16

1 cup	butter, softened	240 mL
1 cup	granulated sugar	240 mL
1 cup	brown sugar	240 mL
2	large eggs	2
1 tsp.	vanilla	5 mL
1 tsp.	baking powder	5 mL
1 tsp.	baking soda	5 mL
2 cups	all-purpose flour	475 mL
1 cup	ground oats (grind to the consistency of coarse bread crumbs)	240 mL
1 lb.	assorted chocolate chips (white, milk, semi-sweet)	455 g
1 cup	chopped pecans (optional)	240 mL

You can buy great-quality white, milk and dark chocolate chips. Only use the best, or it's not worth it! When I buy oats, I grind half in a blender or food processor and keep it in an airtight container to have ready for these cookies. My ten-year-old makes them herself whenever I let her.

Preheat the oven to 350°F (175°C). Grease a baking sheet.

Cream the butter in a large bowl. Add the sugars and stir until well blended. Add the eggs and vanilla.

Sift the baking powder and baking soda with the flour. Add the ground oats to the flour mixture. Add the flour mixture all at once to the butter mixture. Combine thoroughly.

Add the chocolate chips and the nuts, if desired.

Drop by spoonfuls onto the prepared baking sheet. Bake for 10–12 minutes, until golden. Cool on a rack.

muffins & loaves

Low-Fat Pumpkin Cranberry Muffins

Makes 10 to 12

¼ cup	vegetable oil	60 mL
1 cup	brown sugar	240 mL
2	eggs	2
1 cup	buttermilk	240 mL
1 tsp.	vanilla	5 mL
1 cup	pumpkin purée	240 mL
1 cup	all-purpose flour	240 mL
1 cup	whole wheat flour	240 mL
½ tsp.	baking powder	2.5 mL
½ tsp.	baking soda	2.5 mL
1 tsp.	cinnamon	5 mL
½ tsp.	nutmeg	2.5 mL
¼ tsp.	salt	1.2 mL
½ cup	rolled oats	120 mL
½ cup	bran	120 mL
1½ cups	cranberries	360 mL
½ cup	chopped pecans (optional)	120 mL

A great low-fat nutritious muffin.

Preheat the oven to 350°F (175°C). Line a muffin pan with muffin papers or grease with butter.

In a large bowl, mix the oil and brown sugar well. Add the eggs and beat well. Add the buttermilk and vanilla, and mix thoroughly. Stir in the pumpkin purée.

Sift the flours with the baking powder, baking soda, cinnamon, nutmeg and salt. Add the oats and bran. Add the dry ingredients all at once to the buttermilk mixture and mix until just blended.

Fold in the cranberries and the pecans, if desired.

Spoon the batter into the prepared pan, filling the cups ⅔ full. Bake for 25–30 minutes, until a toothpick inserted into the middle comes out clean. Cool in the pan for 10 minutes before removing.

Blueberry Oatmeal Muffins

Makes 10 to 12

⅓ cup	vegetable oil	80 mL
1 cup	brown sugar	240 mL
1 tsp.	vanilla	5 mL
2	eggs	2
1 cup	milk	240 mL
2 cups	flour	475 mL
1 tsp.	baking soda	5 mL
¼ tsp.	baking powder	1.2 mL
1 tsp.	cinnamon	5 mL
½ tsp.	salt	2.5 mL
1 cup	rolled oats	240 mL
1 cup	blueberries	240 mL

Preheat the oven to 350°F (175°C). Line a muffin pan with muffin papers or grease with butter.

In a large bowl, beat the oil, brown sugar, vanilla and eggs together. Add the milk and beat well.

Sift the flour with the baking soda, baking powder, cinnamon and salt. Add the oats and blend well. Add the dry ingredients all at once to the milk mixture and mix until just blended.

Fold in the blueberries.

Spoon the batter into the prepared muffin pan, filling the cups ⅔ full. Bake for 25–30 minutes, until a toothpick inserted into the middle comes out clean. Cool in the pan for 10 minutes before removing.

Another "lower in fat" muffin recipe—you'll love it.

Sun-dried Sour Cherry Muffins

Makes 10 to 12

1⅔ cups	sun-dried sour cherries	400 mL
¾ cup	butter, softened	180 mL
1 cup	brown sugar	240 mL
3	eggs	3
1 tsp.	vanilla	5 mL
3 Tbsp.	milk	45 mL
2 cups	all-purpose flour	475 mL
1¼ tsp.	baking powder	6.2 mL
½ tsp.	baking soda	2.5 mL
½ tsp.	salt	2.5 mL

Try making these with fresh cherries in the summertime! There is no need to soak the fresh fruit.

Preheat the oven to 350°F (175°C). Line a muffin pan with muffin papers or grease with butter.

Cover the sour cherries with hot water and soak for 15 minutes. Drain the cherries and set aside.

In a large bowl, beat the butter and sugar until light and fluffy. Add the eggs one at a time, beating well. Add the vanilla and milk.

Sift the flour with the baking powder, baking soda and salt. Add the dry ingredients all at once to the wet ingredients and mix until just blended.

Gently fold the cherries into the batter.

Spoon the batter into the prepared pan, filling the cups ⅔ full. Bake for 25–30 minutes, until a toothpick inserted into the middle comes out clean. Cool in the pan for 10 minutes before removing.

Raspberry and Blueberry Cornmeal Muffins

Makes 12 muffins

3	eggs	3
1 cup	buttermilk	240 mL
6 Tbsp.	butter, melted	90 mL
½ tsp.	vanilla	2.5 mL
1½ cups	flour	360 mL
1 Tbsp.	baking powder	15 mL
¼ tsp.	cinnamon	1.2 mL
¼ tsp.	nutmeg	1.2 mL
⅓ cup	sugar	80 mL
½ cup	cornmeal	120 mL
1½ cups	blueberries and raspberries combined, rinsed and dried	360 mL

Preheat the oven to 400°F (200°C). Line a muffin pan with muffin papers or grease with butter.

In a large bowl, beat the eggs well. Add the buttermilk and beat thoroughly.

Let the melted butter cool slightly. Blend together with the buttermilk mixture. Stir in the vanilla.

Sift together the flour, baking powder, cinnamon and nutmeg. Add the sugar and cornmeal. Add the dry ingredients all at once to the wet ingredients and mix until just blended. Gently fold the berries into the batter.

Spoon the batter into the prepared pan, filling the cups ¾ full. Bake for 25 minutes, until firm and golden and a toothpick inserted in the center comes out clean. Cool in the pan for 10 minutes before removing.

These are best eaten warm! When I have guests staying overnight, I pre-measure the wet and dry ingredients the night before. In the morning, I mix them with the berries so that we have fresh warm muffins with practically no effort.

Hawaiian Muffins

Makes 12

2 cups	flour	475 mL
1 Tbsp.	baking powder	15 mL
¾ cup	sugar	180 mL
½ tsp.	salt	2.5 mL
2	eggs	2
¾ cup	milk	180 mL
¼ cup	vegetable oil	60 mL
1½ cups	crushed, drained pineapple	360 mL
1 cup	sweetened shredded coconut	240 mL

This is the latest addition to our repertoire. Hope you like these as much as I do!

Preheat the oven to 350°F (175°C). Line a muffin pan with muffin papers or grease with butter.

In a large bowl, sift the flour, baking powder, sugar and salt together.

Combine the eggs, milk and oil and mix into the dry ingredients. Stir until just blended. Add the pineapple and coconut.

Spoon the batter into the prepared pan, filling the cups ¾ full. Bake for 20–25 minutes, until firm and golden and a toothpick inserted in the center comes out clean. Remove and let cool for 10 minutes before removing.

Cinnamon Sour Cream Coffee Loaf

Makes 1 loaf

1½ cups	sour cream	360 mL
½ Tbsp.	baking soda	7.5 mL
3 cups	all-purpose flour	720 mL
½ Tbsp.	baking powder	7.5 mL
¾ cup	butter, softened	180 mL
1½ cups	granulated sugar	360 mL
3	eggs	3
1½ cups	brown sugar	360 mL
1 Tbsp.	cinnamon	15 mL
¾ cup	ground walnuts	180 mL

Preheat the oven to 350°F (175°C). Grease a 9- x 5-inch (23- x 12.5-cm) loaf pan with butter.

In a bowl, combine the sour cream and baking soda. In another bowl, combine the flour and baking powder.

In a large bowl, cream the butter and granulated sugar together. Beat in the eggs one at a time, until well blended.

Add the sour cream mixture and flour mixture alternately to the butter-sugar mixture, beating until smooth.

Combine the brown sugar, cinnamon and ground walnuts.

Spread half the batter on the bottom of the prepared pan. Sprinkle with half the sugar mixture. Cover with the remainder of the batter and top with the remaining sugar mixture.

Bake for 30–40 minutes, until a tester inserted in the center comes out clean. Remove from the pan and cool before serving.

Grandma Faye's famous coffee cake can be served at breakfast, for a snack or as a brunch dessert.

Lemon Poppyseed Loaf

Makes 1 loaf

2¼ cups	all-purpose flour	535 mL
½ Tbsp.	baking powder	7.5 mL
¾ cup	butter, softened	180 mL
1½ cups	sugar	360 mL
3	eggs	3
1½ Tbsp.	grated lemon rind	22.5 mL
¼ cup	poppyseeds	60 mL
1 cup	milk	240 mL
6 Tbsp.	honey	90 mL
½ cup	sugar	120 mL
2 Tbsp.	lemon juice	30 mL

This is a popular breakfast loaf, sweet and tart all at the same time.

Preheat the oven to 350°F (175°C). Grease a 9- x 5-inch (23- x 12.5-cm) loaf pan with butter.

In a bowl, combine the flour and baking powder. Set aside.

In a large bowl, cream the butter and 1½ cups (360 mL) sugar. Add the eggs one at a time, beating until well blended. Add the grated lemon rind and poppyseeds.

Add the milk alternately with the flour mixture to the butter mixture, blending until smooth.

Pour the batter into the prepared pan. Bake for 1 hour or until a tester inserted in the center comes out clean.

While the loaf is baking, combine the honey, ½ cup (120 mL) sugar and lemon juice.

Remove the loaf from the oven and cool slightly, about 5 minutes. Remove it from the pan and drizzle with the honey-lemon glaze.

Cranberry Orange Loaf

Makes 1 loaf

1 cup	butter, softened	240 mL
¾ cup	sugar	180 mL
4	eggs	4
1½ cups	sifted cake flour	360 mL
2 tsp.	baking powder	10 mL
½ tsp.	salt	2.5 mL
¼ cup	freshly squeezed orange juice	60 mL
1 cup	cranberries, coarsely chopped	240 mL
⅓ cup	whole cranberries	80 mL
3 Tbsp.	lemon juice	45 mL
¼ cup	sugar	60 mL

Preheat the oven to 350°F (175°C). Grease a 9- x 5-inch (23- x 12.5-cm) loaf pan with butter.

In a large bowl, cream the butter and sugar until smooth. Add the eggs one at a time, beating until blended.

In a separate bowl, combine the flour, baking powder and salt. Stir the flour mixture into the butter mixture, alternating with the orange juice and ending with the flour. Beat after each addition until smooth. Fold in the chopped cranberries.

Pour the batter into the prepared pan. Smooth the top and bake for 1 hour, or until a tester inserted in the center comes out clean.

To make the glaze, combine the whole cranberries, lemon juice and ¼ cup (60 mL) sugar in a saucepan over medium heat. Cook until the cranberries are soft, about 5–7 minutes. Crush the cranberries until the glaze is smooth.

Remove the loaf from the oven and cool slightly before removing it from the pan. Spread the glaze over the top of the loaf.

This cranberry loaf is best when made with fresh cranberries, but frozen ones will also work well.

pantry

Vegetable Stock

Makes 8 cups (2 L)

3	onions, coarsely chopped	3
1	bunch celery, coarsely chopped	1
3	medium carrots, coarsely chopped	3
2	potatoes, peeled and coarsely chopped	2
3	tomatoes	3
2	leeks, coarsely chopped	2
½ cup	split peas or lentils	120 mL
4	cloves garlic	4
4–5	peppercorns	4–5
2	bay leaves	2
9 cups	water	2.25 L

In a large stockpot, combine all ingredients and bring to a boil. Simmer slowly for about 2 hours. Remove from the heat and cool. Strain and store in the fridge for up to 10 days or freeze for up to 4 months.

Chicken Stock

Makes 8 cups (2 L)

6 lbs.	chicken backs and necks	2.7 kg
3 cups	coarsely chopped onions	720 mL
2 cups	coarsely chopped carrots	475 mL
2 cups	coarsely chopped celery	475 mL
2 cups	coarsely chopped leeks	475 mL
2	bay leaves	2
4–5	peppercorns	4–5
12 cups	water	3 L

In a large stockpot, sauté the chicken pieces, onions, carrots, celery, leeks, bay leaves and peppercorns. Cover with water and bring to a boil. Simmer for 3–4 hours, skimming off any fat. Remove from the heat and cool. Strain and store in the fridge for up to 1 week or freeze for up to 4 months.

Fish Stock

Makes 8 cups (2 L)

5 lbs.	fish bones (use white fish only, preferably cod and halibut)	2.25 kg
2	medium white onions, coarsely chopped	2
3	stalks celery, coarsely chopped	3
2	leeks, coarsely chopped	2
10 cups	water	2.4 L
3	bay leaves	3
6–7	black peppercorns	6–7
2	bunches parsley, stems only	2

Place the bones, onions, celery and leeks in a large stockpot and cover with water. Add the bay leaves, peppercorns and parsley and bring to a boil. Simmer for about 45 minutes to an hour. Strain through cheesecloth. Store in the fridge for up to 4 days or in the freezer for 1 month.

Beef Stock

Makes 8 cups (2 L)

6½ lbs.	beef bones	3 kg
2 cups	red wine	475 mL
2 cups	coarsely chopped carrots	475 mL
2 cups	coarsely chopped celery	475 mL
4 cups	coarsely chopped onions	950 mL
4 Tbsp.	tomato paste	60 mL
2	bay leaves	2
2	cloves garlic	2
1 Tbsp.	black peppercorns	15 mL
24 cups	water	6 L

Preheat the oven to 400°F (200°C).

Cook the bones in a roasting pan for 1 hour, or until golden brown. Remove the bones to a large stockpot and set aside.

Drain the fat from the roasting pan and place over medium heat. Deglaze the pan with the red wine, scraping the bottom to loosen the browned bits. Pour the liquid into the stockpot and add the remaining ingredients, and enough water to cover. Bring to a boil and simmer for 6–8 hours, periodically skimming off any fat that has risen to the surface.

Remove from the heat and cool. Strain and refrigerate for up to 1 week. It will keep frozen for up to 4 months.

Demi-glace

Makes 4 cups (1 L)

8 cups	beef stock	2 L

Bring the stock to a boil and simmer until reduced by half, about 1½–2 hours. Cool and freeze in 1-cup (250-mL) containers (such as yogurt tubs) until needed.

Salsa

Makes 4 cups (950 mL)

⅛	medium red onion, cut into small dice	⅛
1	clove garlic, crushed	1
1 Tbsp.	chipotle chiles (available in the Mexican section of most grocery stores)	15 mL
¼	bunch cilantro, chopped	¼
4 cups	diced tomatoes	950 mL
1 Tbsp.	sugar	15 mL
1 tsp.	salt	5 mL
1 tsp.	lemon juice	5 mL

Combine all the ingredients and process with a hand blender or food processor until the desired consistency is reached. The sauce will keep for up to a week in the fridge.

Pesto

Makes 3 cups (720 mL)

2 cups	fresh basil, tightly packed	475 mL
1½ cups	olive oil	360 mL
⅓ cup	pine nuts, toasted	120 mL
¾ cup	grated Parmesan cheese	180 mL
1½ tsp.	salt and freshly ground black pepper, combined	7.5 mL
1 tsp.	chopped garlic	5 mL

Combine all the ingredients in a food processor and process into a paste. Pesto can be refrigerated for up to a week or frozen for up to 3 months.

Peanut Sauce

Makes 2 cups (475 mL)

1	medium onion, cut into ¼-inch (.6-cm) dice	1
2	cloves garlic, minced	2
2 Tbsp.	vegetable oil	30 mL
2 Tbsp.	sambal oelek (available in Asian markets)	30 mL
2 Tbsp.	lemon juice	30 mL
2 Tbsp.	soy sauce	30 mL
3 Tbsp.	ketjap manis (sweet soy sauce, available in Asian markets)	45 mL
½ cup	peanut butter (use a smooth, unsweetened type)	120 mL
½–¾ cup	hot water	120–180 mL

In a saucepan over low-medium heat, sauté the onion and garlic in the oil.

Whisk in the sambal oelek, lemon juice, soy sauce, ketjap manis and peanut butter. Whisk in ½ cup (120 mL) of the hot water, and bring to a boil. If the consistency is too thick for dipping, whisk in enough water to thin it out. The sauce can be stored in the fridge for up to 2 weeks.

Toasting Nuts

This method works for almonds, walnuts, hazelnuts, macadamia nuts and pine nuts. Toast all nuts on a cookie sheet in a preheated 375°F (190°C) oven. To ensure that all pieces are toasted, do not pack them too tightly on the sheet. Toast to a light golden color, about 6–8 minutes for 2 cups (475 mL) of nuts.

For hazelnuts, which need to be peeled, the way that seems to work best is to cool them slightly, place the nuts in a towel and rub vigorously. The skins will remain on the towel.

Toasting Cumin

To toast cumin, place 4 Tbsp. (60 mL) whole cumin in a small sauté pan over medium heat. Cook for about 4 minutes, stirring constantly.

Cool and grind in a spice mill or a coffee mill reserved for spice and/or nut grinding. Store for up to a month in your spice cupboard.

Roasting Peppers

Preheat the oven to 400°F (200°C). Wash the peppers. Toss them with olive oil. Place them on a baking sheet. Bake, turning a couple of times, until the peppers are softened, about 12–15 minutes. Remove from the oven and quickly transfer to a bowl. Cover with plastic wrap and let sit for 15 minutes. Peel the skins off the peppers and discard.

Barbecue Sauce

Makes 4 cups (1 L)

2 tsp.	vegetable oil	10 mL
1 cup	finely chopped onions	240 mL
2	cloves garlic, chopped	2
¾ Tbsp.	ground toasted cumin	11 mL
1 tsp.	cayenne pepper	5 mL
½ cup	balsamic vinegar	120 mL
½ cup	red wine vinegar	120 mL
½ cup	soy sauce	120 mL
⅓ cup	brown sugar	80 mL
½ cup	Worcestershire sauce	120 mL
1 tsp.	hot pepper sauce	5 mL
2 cups	ketchup	475 mL

In a large pot, heat the oil and sauté the onions until golden brown, about 10 minutes. Add the remaining ingredients, except for the ketchup. Simmer about 30 minutes until the desired consistency is reached. The sauce should be reduced by about ⅔. Remove from the heat. Allow to cool to room temperature. Add the ketchup and blend with a hand blender. The sauce will keep in the fridge for up to 2 weeks.

Blackened Spice Mix

Makes 6 Tbsp. (90 mL)

1 Tbsp.	cayenne pepper	15 mL
2 Tbsp.	chili powder	30 mL
2 Tbsp.	paprika	30 mL
2 tsp.	ground thyme	10 mL
½ tsp.	freshly ground black pepper	2.5 mL
½ tsp.	salt	2.5 mL
2 tsp.	ground oregano	10 mL

Thoroughly mix all the ingredients together. Store in an airtight container for up to 1 month.

Parsley Oil

Makes 1½ cups (360 mL)

2 cups	fresh parsley leaves	475 mL
1 cup	cilantro	240 mL
1½ cups	olive oil	360 mL

Blanch the parsley and cilantro in boiling water for 15–20 seconds. Strain quickly and plunge into ice water. Drain in a strainer or colander and press gently to squeeze out excess moisture.

In a blender, purée the parsley and cilantro with the olive oil. Let sit for 24 hours at room temperature. Strain and store for up to 1 week in the fridge.

Rosemary Oil

Makes 2 cups (475 mL)

| 2 cups | rosemary leaves | 475 mL |
| 1½ cups | olive oil | 360 mL |

Blanch the rosemary in boiling salted water for 30–40 seconds. Drain and plunge in ice water to stop it from cooking any further. Drain in a strainer or colander and press gently to squeeze out excess moisture.

In a blender, process the rosemary and olive oil. Let sit for 24 hours at room temperature. Strain and store in the fridge for up to 1 week.

Cilantro Oil

Makes 1 cup (240 mL)

3	bunches cilantro	3
1	bunch parsley	1
1 cup	olive oil	120 mL
1 tsp.	salt	5 mL

Blanch the cilantro and parsley in boiling water for 15–30 seconds. Drain and plunge into ice water. Drain in a strainer or colander and press gently to squeeze out excess moisture.

Using a blender, purée the cilantro, parsley, oil and salt. Let sit for 24 hours at room temperature. Strain and store in the fridge for up to 1 week.

Basil Oil

Makes 1¾ cups (420 mL)

2 cups	basil leaves	475 mL
1 cup	parsley	240 mL
¾ cup	olive oil	180 mL
¾ cup	canola oil	180 mL

Blanch the basil and parsley in boiling water for 15–30 seconds. Drain and plunge into ice water. Drain in a strainer or colander and press gently to squeeze out excess moisture.

Using a blender, purée the basil, parsley, olive oil and canola oil. Let sit for 24 hours at room temperature. Strain and store in the fridge for up to 1 week.

Crème Fraîche

Makes 1½ cups (360 mL)

1 cup	whipping cream	240 mL
½ cup	sour cream	120 mL

Blend both ingredients in a small saucepan and heat until lukewarm, about 105–110°F (40–43°C).

Place in a bowl and cover with a damp cloth. Keep in a warm area of the kitchen for about 24 hours, then refrigerate. May be kept in the fridge for up to a week.

Index

Index

Index

Index

Index

Index

Index

Index

Index

Index

Index